IB PSYCHOLOGY HIGHER LEVEL

International Baccalaureate

Revision Guide

Jacob Solomon

Getting the most out of this book...

Dear .... (write your first name here),

This book is written for you, the IB student in psychology.

The purpose of studying psychology is to interact with other people and situations at a deeper, more comprehending, and better-informed level. It may even lead you to a career and to your life's calling. In the meantime, you have to pass IB psychology. These notes are put together to help you to do just that.

This book is designed specifically to help you to review the material of the course. The word revision literally means to see again. By presenting the material in brief, review form, you should get the overall feel and perspective of how the topics you have studied come together. That includes their perspectives, wide variety of methods used, and how the ideas and findings relate to one another. In short, you should see the wood, despite the trees.

The reality of the IB psychology exam is that you are expected to recall and apply a large data-base of theory, methodology, and research studies. Though there is considerable material on each area of the IB syllabus, this book refers to the theory and research commonly selected and used in the IB psychology program. **It has endeavored to select as review material from the theory and research that you are most likely to have come across in classes and in reading assignments.**

Please e-mail me care of osc@osc-ib-com with any suggestions for inclusion in later editions of this work.

If this review book has helped you pass your exam, I'm happy. If it has increased your clarity in psychology, I'm delighted. And if it helped you to know yourself a little better, I'm thrilled.

My thanks go to Mrs. Susan Hirsch, and Ms. Brittany Browning for advising and checking the text. Also to my ex-students, especially Mr. Adam Mayes, for advice and assistance.

Wishing you every success! (But remember that success comes before work in the dictionary only.)

Jacob Solomon

RECOMMENDED STUDY TEXTS FOR IB PSYCHOLOGY

Crane, J. & Hannibal, J. (2009) IB Diploma Program. Psychology Course Companion. Oxford University Press.

Hannibal, J. (2012) IB Study Guide. Psychology for the IB Diploma. Oxford University Press.

Law, A. Halkiopoulos, C. & Bryan-Zaykov C. (2010) Pearson Baccalaureate. Psychology. Developed specifically for the IB Diploma. Pearson Education Ltd.

CONTENTS

Chapter 1	The biological level of analysis	4
Chapter 2	The cognitive level of analysis	14
Chapter 3	The socio-cultural level of analysis	24
Chapter 4	Abnormal psychology	39
Chapter 5	Development psychology	56
Chapter 6	Health psychology	71
Chapter 7	Human relationships	86
Chapter 8	Sports psychology	99
Chapter 9	Qualitative Methodology in psychology	115
Checklist for the internal assessment…		126

CHAPTER ONE – THE BIOLOGICAL LEVEL OF ANALYSIS

Paper 1 – core topic

Our cognitions, emotions and behaviors are products of our nervous and endocrine systems. **Biological issues of interest to psychologists include:**

- Different areas of the brain carry out different functions.
- Synapses (gaps) exist between nerve cells. Different neurotransmitters carry different neural transmissions (messages) from one synapse to another, according to our psychological functioning.
- The role of hormones in our psychological functioning.

The biological level of analysis thus emphasizes that cognitions, emotions and behaviors are products of our nervous and endocrine systems.

New brain imaging technologies (for example, CAT (computerized axial tomography), PET (positron emission tomography), and fMRI (functional magnetic resonance imaging), have made it possible to study living brains in action as various tasks are performed. This makes it possible, for example, to correlate specific areas of brain damage with specific changes in a person's personality or cognitive abilities. The key word is correlate. We know relatively little of the actual changes that take place within the brain. We do not have the capacity to view a piece of brain tissue and read the knowledge contained therein.

Advances in psychopharmacology (the study of medicine that addresses the balance of chemicals in the brain) have led to the development of new medications for conditions such as depression, and eating disorders. These are considered in the option: 'Abnormal Psychology'.

The biological perspective incorporates the theory of the evolutionary process. It takes into account the survival of the fittest. Indeed, those who adapt to environmental changes and challenges are those who get the best opportunities to mate and pass their adaptive genes to the next generation. The rest tend to die out.

Behavioral genetics considers that behavior patterns can be inherited. It applies biological analysis to understand and explain differences in individual people's conduct.

METHODS USED IN THE BIOLOGICAL LEVEL OF ANALYSIS INCLUDE:

1. Laboratory experiments (exemplified by Baumgartner 2008 below, on the role of oxytocin on economic decision making). This involves a test sample and a control sample to determine the acceptance or rejection of a hypothesis. The conditions are the same except that the IV (independent variable) is different in the test sample. The control sample may use a placebo: where the control participants are deceived in being told that they are in the experimental condition, where in fact they are not (e.g. given tonic water and told that it contains vodka, and then tested for driving reactions after that drink). The main criticism of the placebo or any type of blind condition is ethical: deception at various levels is involved. The ethical issues may be reduced by debriefing the participants at the end of the study.

2. Correlation studies, exemplified by Perry 1997 below, on the effect of deprivation on neuro-plasticity). Based on brain scans, he found a positive correlation between the size of the brain and child neglect. The ethical issues are reduced by the child neglect having been in the past.

3. Case studies: exemplified by the brain damage cases of HM, and Clive Wearing, below. These do not involve any clinical interference, but rely solely on findings that were made after the brain damage took place. The ethical issues are like the correlation studies, above. In addition, the uniqueness of the details of the cases would need greater safeguards to the participants' anonymity.

BIOLOGICAL LEVEL OF ANALYSIS: STRENGTHS.

- High credibility – scientifically-based subject matter and its experimental methodology.
- Effective practical applications – e.g. the use of medication in treating mental conditions.
- Contributes to an understanding a wide range of phenomena – e.g. why people fall in love.
- Nature based – strong arguments favoring the nature side of the nature/nurture debate.

BIOLOGICAL LEVEL OF ANALYSIS: WEAKNESSES.

- Reductionist – could overlook interactions with environmental factors that also affect people's behavior.
- Determinist – can lead to e.g. explaining criminal behavior in terms of individual physiology, and genes: "It wasn't me, it was my nervous system".
- Nature based – lacks sufficient recognition of the nurture side of the nature/nurture debate.

A. Physiology and behavior

Explain one study related to localization of function in the brain *(for example, Kim and Hirsch).*

The case of railway worker Phineas Gage (1848) showed that brain functions are localized: an explosion sent a pole right through his brain. He lost some, but not all his mental capacities – demonstrating that different parts of the brain have different functions. The parts of the brain having specific functions are becoming clearer with modern methods of brain scanning, exemplified by:

Kim and Hirsch (1997) used fMRI (functional magnetic resonance imaging) to see **how the brain processes language in bilingual people.** One group had learned a second language as children. The other had learned a second language later in life. Both groups had to think about what they had done the day before – first in one language, and then in the other.

Kim and Hirsch investigated the Broca's area - in the left frontal lobe of the brain, which manages speech production, and the Wernicke's area - in the rear of the brain, which processes the meaning of language. Both groups of people used the same part of the Wernicke's area no matter what language they were speaking. But their use of the Broca's area differed. Those who learned a second language as children used the same region in the Broca's area for speaking both languages. But those who learned a second language later in life made use of a distinct additional region in Broca's area for their second language, close to the one activated for their native tongue.

This suggests that language is being hard-wired during early childhood development. Once that wiring is complete, the management of a new language must be handled by a different part of the brain.

Thus it appears from this research that (a) the part of the brain used for language learning is indeed localized (b) knowing more than one language from childhood does not affect efficacy in either, and (c) learning to speak a language later in life requires much more brain activity.

Evaluation: strengths

(a) Scanning appears to confirm that both the Broca's and the Wernicke's areas do serve distinct and specialized functions in language comprehension and in speech production.
(b) It helps to explain why post-childhood learners of a foreign language tend to make errors based on mother-tongue influence.

Evaluation: weaknesses

(a) Differences in language-learning ability may be connected with the way the learner interacts with the language. Mothers teaching an infant to speak are very tactile, auditory, and visual. High school foreign language teachers tend to be less so.
(b) Early learners do not bring to language learning the fears of learning vocabulary and grammar.

Using one or more examples, explain effects of neurotransmission on human behavior.

Neurotransmitters are substances found in the terminal buttons of a neuron (nerve cell), and are biochemical in structure. They enable stimuli (such as pricking your finger on a red rose) to be processed and reacted to by the central nervous system (brain and spinal cord). Neurons are not joined together in one long chain, but each one is separated from the adjacent ones by synaptic clefts (gaps between the nerve cells).

Communication between neurons is an electro/biochemical process. The neural impulse is electric, which stimulates the release of the neurotransmitters. These jump across the synaptic clefts, and are absorbed by the receptor cells of the receptors (dendrites) of one or more adjacent neurons. This process repeats itself from neuron to neuron, and to / from / within the central nervous system (brain and spinal cord).

A person's biological and psychological situation can affect the rate of release (the 'firing') of neurotransmitters. Drugs such as alcohol and nicotine can stimulate neurotransmitter activity, and also inhibit neurotransmitter activity by covering the ends of the synaptic site. Any one neuron may be working with some 10,000 synapses from many thousands of other neurons.

Dopamine is a neurotransmitter that helps to control the brain's reward and pleasure centers. Increased dopamine levels in the brain mean increased stimulation. For happy experiences, dopamine release sets the pleasure circuit in action. Dopamine is manufactured in the brain, in the nerve cell bodies located within the ventral tegmental area (VTA), and is released in the nucleus accumbens and the prefrontal cortex.

Dopamine is 'fired' when, for example, you see a Coca-Cola advertisement and you immediately get the pleasure that you associate with that drink - without taking any of it.

Dopamine is also partly responsible for nicotine addiction. Nicotine stimulates adrenaline hormones, causing increased heartbeat, which in turn creates feelings of pleasure with the release of the dopamine neurotransmitters. Those feelings also stimulate acetylcholine neurotransmitters, creating more acetylcholine receptors sites in the process.

Withdrawal means that these newly-formed receptor sites yearn for neurotransmitters, resulting in a craving for more cigarettes. That is what makes smoking not easy to give up.

The work of Fisher (2004) on a sample of newly-fallen-in-love couples demonstrated that both dopamine and serotonin (below) levels are very high. This was reflected in their behavior: less need for food and sleep, and could not get their minds off even the tiniest detail of the new partner. Craving for each other's company caused the same emotional rush of pleasure on meeting as a fix of cocaine for a drug addict (Fisher, 2004).

Seratonin is an inhibitory neurotransmitter, employed by the nervous system in mediation of pain, sleep control, and regulation of mood. High levels of serotonin are associated with feelings of well-being and happiness, and of being at peace with the world.

Seratonin is also associated with hallucinating. Kasamatsu & Hirai (1999) studied how physical deprivation affects the brain. Their participants were a group of Buddhist monks on pilgrimage to a holy mountain in Japan, exposed to the cold and going without food and water for two days. The monks then perceived the presence of their ancestors. The researchers found that the hallucinations were a product of the increased serotonin level in the monks' brains, especially in the hypothalamus and frontal cortex.

Using one or more examples, explain the functions of two hormones in human behavior.

Hormones are chemicals released by the various ductless glands (e.g. adrenal gland, pineal gland) and are carried through the blood system to where they are most needed. Some hormones can also act as neurotransmitters (above), such as dopamine and oxytocin.

OXYTOCIN: Romantic love according to the anthropological research of Fisher (2004) is not an emotion, but a hormone-based motivation system. This can create a craving, to enable lovers to mate, feel very close to each other, and produce offspring. Oxytocin is released with touches and hugs, especially in sex.

Oxytocin is secreted by the hypothalamus and released in two ways: (a) through the pituitary gland into the bloodstream functioning as a hormone, and (b) into the central nervous system (brain and spinal cord) where it connects with oxytocin receptors – functioning as a neurotransmitter.

The experimental study of Baumgartner et al (2008) investigated the function of oxytocin as an active hormone in economic decision-making - aimed to investigate the role of oxytocin (IV – independent variable) in causing a cheated partner to forgive and continue the trust that had existed in the relationship (DV - dependent variable).

The test group was given an oxytocin supplement, and the control group a placebo. Both groups then played a trust game. The 'investor' players received a sum of money which they were told to either keep or share with a second 'trustee' player. If the sum was shared, it would be tripled. The 'trustee' player could share the money (trust), or could keep the money (betrayal). The participants played against different 'second players' in the trust game, and then against a computer in a similar risk game. The trust was betrayed in half the games. The players received feedback at once from those conducting the experiment. Those who had taken oxytocin continued to invest (forgave, continued to trust despite betrayal) at the same rate when playing with people (but not the computer), even though they knew that they had been cheated. Those on the placebo invested less.

fMRI brain scans showed that the test group showed a decreased response in the highly-concentrated oxytocin receptor amygdala section of the brain, and in the caudate nucleus in the brain (involved in reward-related responses, and learning to trust).

Evaluation: strengths

(a) Experimental nature of study.
(b) Shows biological input to people forgiving and restoring trust within relationships.
(c) Can show why being in love may blind to very serious faults in one's partner.

Evaluation: limitations

(a) The areas of the brain scanned did show decreased action, but the connection with oxytocin was entirely correlational. There was no scientific explanation of the physiological work of oxytocin supplement.
(b) The effects of nasal spray oxytocin, and naturally produced oxytocin may differ.

MELATONIN, produced by the pineal gland, is secreted as a reaction to the dark, and inhibited by light. It affects human behavior in helping us to sleep. Its precise function is to communicate with the pituitary gland, which in turn sends out other hormones which make it difficult to stay awake. Thus people tend to sleep more during the long winter nights than in the shorter summer nights, and less if there is a light on in the bedroom.

SAD (seasonal affective disorder) is a type of depression occurring at the beginning and end of winter, which seems to be related to melatonin levels. Associated behaviors include fatigue, irritability, problems concentrating, loss of sex-drive, and insomnia.

The work of Avery et al. (2001) demonstrated the function of melatonin in the behaviors of 95 SAD patients, divided into three groups. The first received 'dawn simulation' – an artificial-lighting-produced false dawn starting at 4:30 am (involving timing the bedroom lights to come on gradually during the hour or so before awakening). The second was given bright light therapy, and the third a placebo dim red light at dawn. That last group was put under the impression that the dim red light would help their SAD symptoms. In reality, the dim red light would not have stopped the melatonin secretion and removed the SAD symptoms. Results: those given dawn simulation and bright light therapy were able to fit their sleep patterns with their normal routines by stopping the sleep-promoting melatonin. Dawn simulation was actually more effective: it happened without the side-effects of the headaches and nausea of the bright light therapy group. Those who were given the placebo were not deceived, and in most cases the SAD continued.

Discuss two effects of the environment on physiological processes.

THE EFFECT OF DEPRIVATION ON NEURO-PLASTICITY: the brain adapts to the challenges placed on it by developing appropriate new neurons. For example you might find maths very difficult, but with regular practice, the part of the brain that deals with maths on a challenging basis 'thickens', and handles maths more effectively. Thus the more you exercise your brain, the more powerful it becomes. The dendrites (branches) of the neurons grow in numbers and connect with other neurons.

The work of Perry (1997) compared the brain scans of three-year-olds with normal degrees of human interaction with those suffering extreme neglect. Findings: (a) on the whole, the brains of severely neglected children tend to be smaller than those who had been normally nurtured, and (b) there are large ventricular spaces in the brains of the neglected children, which would interfere with moods, sleep, and regulation of anxiety. Some of the neurons of children lacking social interaction will not make enough connections to remain functional, and will wither.

Thus the lack of early-learning activities and demanding education means an overall poorer life's experience with a less sophisticated and developed brain.

THE EFFECT OF LIGHT ON SLEEP, INDUCED BY THE PRESENCE OR ABSENCE OF MELATONIN - has been linked with SAD: *see above, including the study of Avery et al. (2001).*

Examine one interaction between cognition and physiology in terms of behavior *(for example amnesia).* **Evaluate two relevant studies.**

AMNESIA – HOW BRAIN DAMAGE (BIOLOGICAL) AFFECTS MEMORY PROCESSING (COGNITIVE PROCESS):

Amnesia is the inability to learn new information or retrieve information that has already been stored in the memory. **Anterograde amnesia** is the failure to store memories after brain damage. **Retrograde amnesia** is the failure to recall memories that have been stored before brain damage. The brain damage may be caused by brain injury or infection. In behavioral decision-making, this will mean being cut off from past experiences and/or not being able to act with regard to future consequences of the behavior.

The case of H.M. – suffered head injury at age 9 (in 1957), which cause serious epileptic seizures. Doctors removed the tissue from the temporal lobe of the brain (there was no effective drug treatment at the time), including the hippocampus. Following the operation, HM could recall information acquired early in life, but could not form new memories; a case of anterograde amnesia. HM's brain was scanned in 1997, showing that the areas that had been damaged included the hippocampus and amygdala regions. The fact that HM's memory functioned at all indicated that memory functions are more widely distributed throughout the brain than previously thought, and not just in the hippocampus and amygdala regions.

The case of Clive Wearing (current) - in 1985 Clive Wearing, a distinguished middle-aged English musician and musicologist, suffered a brain infection which interfered with memory. It reduced the memory span to a few seconds – practically living in the very present only. His amnesia was mainly anterograde. He could still perform and conduct the music he knew before the infection. His emotional memory prior to the infection was unaffected: he still loved his wife. This indicates that different memory functions are distributed widely throughout the brain.

Evaluation of studies: These findings are supported by recent studies of the brain showing that the hippocampus stores the explicit long term memory (lifelong, virtually infinite capacity), and the amygdala tends to hold emotional experiences, but the implicit long-term memory (e.g. how to play the piano) would be located elsewhere in the brain, as illustrated by the Clive Wearing case.

Modern brain scanning procedures showed up exactly which areas were affected by HM's operation (the damage turned out to be widespread), and also made it possible to pinpoint the precise nature of the biological damage to Clive Wearing's brain. These studies have the scope of demonstrating which parts of the brain relate to which aspects of human behavior. However:

- The scanners were not used in the natural environment – issue of ecological validity.

- The information scanners' colored light responses may exaggerate the different activities in the brain.
- The brain areas might light up on the machine for reasons other than those supposed by the investigator.

HOW MEDITATION (COGNITIVE) CAN CHANGE BRAIN ACTIVITY AND UNTIMATELY LEAD TO CHANGES IN THE BRAIN STUCTURE (BIOLOGICAL).

The study of Davidson et al. (2004) used an EEG (electroencephalograph) to compare the **gamma waves** (highest-frequency brainwaves, associated with the most intense concentration) of those with established training and experience in **meditation** with those without.

This was achieved by comparing the brain gamma wave activity between eight monks to whom meditation was part of life, and ten students who were given one week of meditation training before the study. For the study, all participants were required to create a deep feeling of compassion without focusing it on any particular person.

The EEG findings showed the monks to have a much better organized and a much higher degree of gamma wave activity. The brains of the students showed only a slight increase in gamma wave activity following the week's training in meditation.

The study suggests that a mind trained in meditation becomes biologically more suited to meditate. It will have a much fuller experience of its potential benefits when applied to relieving stress and physical pain. On a wider basis, this suggests that a mind experienced in any particular skill becomes biologically adapted to carrying out that skill. However:

- The results were entirely correlational: the higher level of gamma waves in the monks' brains may be a product of non-meditation experiences.
- The information scanners' colored light responses may exaggerate the different activities in the brain.
- The brain areas might light up on the machine for reasons other than those supposed by the investigator.

Discuss the use of brain imaging technologies *(for example, CAT, PET, fMRI)* **in investigating the relationship between biological factors and behavior.**

REVIEW THE FOLLOWING STUDIES DESCRIBED EARLIER IN THIS CHAPTER:

MRI (magnetic resonance imaging) and fMRI (functional magnetic resonance imaging) produce three-dimensional images of brain structures, and at the same time have the capacity to record changes in the use of oxygen in the blood. When the brain is more active in e.g. a studying task, it shows the increased oxygen level. Brain imaging technologies were instrumental in many studies including those described previously:

(a) Kim and Hirsch (1997) – on the use of an fMRI in determining the parts of the brain used in language learning at different ages.
(b) Baumgartner et al. (2008) – on the use of an fMRI in investigating the effects of higher concentrations of oxytocin on economic decision-making.
(c) Perry (1997) on use of MRI scans in studying the effect of deprivation of warm social contact on neuroplasticity in young children.
(d) HM (1997) and Clive Wearing on the use of MRI scans to determine the localization of different memory functions in different parts of the brain.
(e) Davidson et al. (2004) on the use of an EEG to measure gamma waves as a means of determining capacities and powers of concentration in meditation.

However, in these studies:

- The scanners were not always used in the natural environment – issue of ecological validity.
- The information scanners' colored light responses may have exaggerated the different activities in the brain.
- The brain areas might have lit up on the machine for reasons other than those supposed by the investigators.

B. Genetics and behavior

With reference to relevant research studies, to what extent does genetic inheritance influence behavior?

Research in this field is currently only empirical, rather than biochemical. That is because we do not currently have the scientific knowledge to identify specific combinations of genes with tendencies towards specific behaviors.

THE RESEARCH OF HUTCHINGS AND MENDICK (1975) ON THE EFFECT OF GENETICS ON CRIMINAL BEHAVIOR is involved in the discussion of whether crime running in families is genetically-based or not.

This research was empirically-based, on adoption situations. It sought to investigate whether criminal behavior was more likely to have been learnt from the adoption environment, or if it was guided by specific genes towards criminal behavior.

This study found that if both the biological and adoptive fathers had criminal records, more than a third of the sons would also get criminal records. If just the biological father had a criminal record, it would drop to about a fifth of the sons getting a criminal record. Where the adoptive father had such a record it dropped to 11%. Where neither father had one (the control), 10% of the sons had a criminal record.

Conclusion: genetics (nature) played a somewhat greater (but certainly not exclusive) role than upbringing (nurture) in influencing criminal behavior. However, the study may be criticized:

- Children who are adopted are often placed in a similar environment to their natural parents.
- Genes seem unlikely to account for criminal behavior peaking in the 20s age-group, and then sharply declining.
- Legal definitions of different types of crime are unlikely to conform to genetic structures.

THE WORK OF SANTTILA ET AL (2008) ON THE EFFECT OF GENETICS ON HOMOSEXUAL BEHAVIORAL TENDENCIES based in Finland, involved an empirically-based study of twins and their siblings: some 6,000 female twins and 3,000 male twins. In order to establish homosexual tendencies, as well as behaviors, the participants responded to a questionnaire including the frequency of same-sex sexual contact in the year before the study. They were also asked whether or not they would agree to intercourse with a physically attractive member of the same sex if nobody would know, there was no access to the opposite sex, and it could be done on the participant's own terms.

The overt incidence of homosexual behavior was 3% for men and just over 1% for women. The potential for homosexual response was much higher: nearly two thirds of the women, and nearly one third of the men stated that there was some chance that they would agree.

The study indicated that both the MZ (monozygotic, one egg and two sperm) and DZ (dizygotic, two eggs and two sperm) twins' concordance rates were significant at the potential level, but only the MZ twins' concordance rates were significant at the overt level. With the MZ twins, the females showed a much higher concordance rate (over 50%) at the overt level, than the males (a little under 40%). However, males and female MZ twins showed a 53% concordance rate at the potential level.

This seems to indicate that homosexual behavior at both the overt level and potential (including fantasy) level has a genetic component.

Evaluation: strengths

(a) Empirical study – large sample in the region of 9,000 twins.
(b) The guaranteed anonymity reduced the possibility that the responses were biased towards demand characteristics (a response that the participants thought that the interviews wanted).

Evaluation: weaknesses

(a) Empirically based: no attempt to discover genetic elements promoting homosexuality.
(b) How they would have acted if faced with the potential situation was speculative.

Examine one evolutionary explanation of behavior.

As a human race, we are all the products of people successful enough to attract a partner who found them so alluring that they wanted to pass their genes to the next generation. Those who failed this 'test' were doomed to extinction. None of them could have been be our ancestors. As only the stronger people tended to produce offspring, the human race appears to have evolved to be stronger, by the survival of the fittest, by evolution.

The work of Wedekind (1995) suggests that the desire to produce healthy children that are resistant to disease is an **evolutionary-based, unconscious factor in our behavior when it comes to choosing a partner.** This is based on MHC (major histo-compatibility complex) - genetic compatibility is behind our choice of partner. We are the product of those MHC genes that are co-dominant, meaning that both sets of inherited genes have an effect on the child's immune system. Thus the more varied the MHC genes of the parents, the stronger the immune systems of the children. With his 'dirty shirt' experiment, he showed that women preferred (and thus would have chosen) the scent of men with dissimilar genes – without knowing the reason why. This involved 49 women and 44 men with a wide range of MSC genes. The men wore the the new t-shirts supplied for two nights in row, and had no contact with anything that might interfere with the natural body odor. The women smelt the returned, unwashed t-shirts. They rated the smells of each t-shirt. Result: women preferred the scent of men with different genes.

Discuss ethical considerations in research into genetic influences on behavior.

The most widespread aim of research in human genetics is to identify particular genes involved in heredity diseases. Its potential for improving the overall quantity and quality of life has to be balanced with the following ethical issues:

(a) Danger of information leaks on 'adverse' genetic characteristics creating difficulties in finding a partner, getting a job, or the terms of a medical insurance policy. The researcher has to guarantee confidentiality, with a signed consent document showing the participant's clear understanding of the study and its implications.
(b) Possibility that a participant has unknowingly has been adopted.
(c) Participant anonymity protects, but can prevent any follow-up study.
(d) The importance of the discovery of a previously unknown genetic disorder might well be over-exaggerated by the participant – or taken out of proportion/context.
(e) Cultural issues are extremely sensitive with many ethnic groups. Typically, the elders of the society must be consulted for permission to work with members of their group.

POSSIBLE EXAMINATION QUESTIONS

SHORT ANSWER QUESTIONS

Outline two principles that define the biological level of analysis.

Examine one evolutionary aspect of behavior.

LONG ANSWER QUESTIONS

Examine one interaction between cognition and physiology in terms of behavior. Evaluate two relevant studies.

With reference to at least one research study, to what extent does genetic inheritance influence behavior?

CHAPTER TWO – THE COGNITIVE LEVEL OF ANALYSIS

Paper 1 – core topic

Cognitive psychology focuses on the way the individual processes information and understands and interacts with the environment. Cognitive psychologists suggest that humans form internal mental representations (schemas) that guide behavior, and they developed a range of research methods to study these. If the mind is like a computer, the brain is the hardware, and the schemas are the software.

The cognitive level of analysis is defined as focusing on "the processes by which the sensory input (e.g. something we read or hear) is transformed, reduced, elaborated, stored, recovered, and used" (Neisser, 1967).

In the mid-1950s, psychologists began to explore cognition to further understanding of human behavior. The focus was shifting from studying observable behavior to studying mental processes, such as memory and perception. It came to include how we interpret information, our emotions, and our behaviors.

Cognitive psychologists use traditional research methods (for example, experiments and verbal protocols) but there is an increasing emphasis on the use of modern technology which gives biological rather than direct cognitive information, such as PET, CAT, MRI, and fMRI scans.

Today, cognitive psychologists increasingly work together with neuroscientists, social psychologists and cultural psychologists. They recognize that the cognitive approach interacts in many ways with biological and socio-cultural phenomena. Cognitive psychologists also work on the following premises:

(a) *The way we mentally process things guides our behavior.* We do not see a reality or situation objectively. Instead, we take the input environment and process the information into a mental representation. This brings in our stores of related knowledge and experience, and our own individualized, culturally-influenced schemas. Our reactions, guided by those mental representations, are the output. (Differences in mental representation come up when you discuss a movie with a friend and find that you both got a very different impression of it. This is exemplified in Bartlett's study, below. See also LeDoux's model near the end of this chapter - a very different study on how the way we mentally process things guides our behavior.)

(b) *The way we mentally process things should be studied scientifically.* That can involve experimental studies, whose findings generate empirical evidence. This is exemplified by the laboratory experiment of Loftus and Palmer below, on reconstructive memory.

METHODS USED AT THE COGNITIVE LEVEL OF ANALYSIS INCLUDE:

1. Laboratory experiments (exemplified by Anderson and Pichert 1978, below, on whether schema processing affects both encoding and retrieval of information). This involves a test sample and a control sample to determine the acceptance or rejection of a hypothesis. The conditions are the same except that the IV (independent variable) is changed in the test sample only.

2. The use of neuro-technology to trace the intensity of an emotion, and its path through the brain. For example, when given a series of products and being required to rate their attractiveness (see Kilts' use of MRI brain imaging in his study of product preferences near the end of this chapter).

3. Case studies: exemplified by the brain damage cases of HM, and Clive Wearing in this and the previous chapter. These are focused on amnesia – how brain damage (biological factor) affects memory processing (cognitive process).

In an exam, expand these studies where relevant.

ETHICAL CONSIDERATIONS: similar to those in the biological approach, including:

(a) Informed consent – participants must know the object of the study, that their involvement is voluntary, what the data will be used for, and if necessary be debriefed at the end of the study. In extreme cases, the ethical requirement for informed consent might be waived, when the focus of the study is of public importance and there is no other way to obtain the information.
(b) Making the participants anonymous to protect them, even at the risk of reducing the authenticity of the research and of preventing any follow-up study.
(c) Bearing in mind that cognitive research involving associated cultural issues is extremely sensitive with many ethnic groups. Typically, the elders of the society must be consulted for permission to work with members of their group.

A. Cognitive processes

Evaluate schema theory with reference to research studies.

A cognitive schema is a network of knowledge, beliefs, and expectations about particular aspects of the world. These are built up through our own experiences of life, education, and culture. Examples of schemas are the capacity to communicate in English, pick up on the teacher's mood, and to drink out of a cup without leaving a mess. Cognitive psychology operates on the assumption that our developing schemas guide our behavior.

Where recalling realities of a situation that interfere with the person's existing schema, the mind tends to reconstruct what happened along the lines of the schema, even though it could well be incorrect. This is **reconstructive memory**, as illustrated by the classic research of **Bartlett (1932)**. The participants (people with a British western socio-cultural background) were required to read a short 329-word story "The War of the Ghosts" that was based on a Native American legend. They were not told the purpose of the experiment. After 15 minutes, Bartlett asked the participants to reproduce the story from memory. He found that as the story was reproduced, it became shorter and more conventional (in retaining only the details that western cultural schemas could relate to), but still coherent.

Bartlett concluded that people reconstruct the past by trying to fit it into existing schemas – even though it can involve imaginative, but inaccurate reconstruction of the experience.

The notion that memory is reconstructive has been supported by the classic study of Loftus and Palmer (1974). This experiment involved 45 students who were shown movies of traffic accidents. They had to recall details on the speed of the cars when the accident took place.

In this experiment, the critical question was: 'How fast were the cars going when they hit each other?' The hypothesis was that when the question was alternatively phrased with different groups, the more emphatic the word in this question, the faster the cars would have been 'recalled' to be going. In separate trials, the word 'hit' was replaced with 'smashed' 'collided' 'bumped' 'contacted'. The hypothesis was that leading questions (questions that in some way suggest the response) and post-event information influence schema processing, which may affect the accuracy of recall.

The results indicated a significant support for the hypothesis. 'Smashed' 'collided' and 'bumped' got significantly faster speed estimates than 'hit' and 'contacted'. The conclusion was that different words activate different schemas in the memory, so that hearing the word 'smashed' caused the memory to reconstruct a more severe picture than hearing the word 'contacted'.

The notion that schema processing affects retrieval from the memory store as well as encoding into the memory store been supported by the classic study of Anderson and Pichert (1978). This experiment involved two groups of people at the first stage, which became four groups of people at the second stage.

In the first stage, they were divided into two groups: one was to think in the framework (schema) of a house-purchaser, and the other in the framework of a house-breaker (burglar). Both groups heard a story about two boys who missed school and went to one of their homes, knowing that it was always empty on Thursdays. The story contained a total of 72 points for recall, including that the roof was leaky and the basement was damp. Also, the house contained a color-TV, a ten-geared bicycle, and a valuable coin collection. The groups were given a short distraction task and then each member of the group had to recall as many points as possible.

In the second stage, half the house-buyer sample was given the house-breaker schema, and half the house-breaker sample was given the house-buyer schema. The other halves kept the same schema as in the first stage. There were thus four groups in all.

The two groups that retained the first schema recalled fewer points the second time round. The two groups that changed schemas the second time round recalled 7% more points in total, with 10% more directly related to their new schemas. Recall in points related to their original first schema declined.

This controlled study indicates that schema processing affects retrieval from the memory store as well as encoding into the memory store, because those with changed schemas relied entirely on what they heard at the beginning of the first stage. The study may be criticized on its laboratory setting (lacked ecological validity), but it may be supported in that there was a controlled situation which highlighted effective retrieval from the memory store as the sole source of information for recall.

Evaluation of schema theory – strengths:

(a) Helps to understand social issues such as bias and prejudice. Schema theory explains how a person who witnesses an incident turns it to fit in with what he already believes and feels he knows.
(b) Schema interference explains people's failure to remember and report information accurately. The schema lies at the base of people's natural scope to reconstruct memory. It reflects the brain's search for meaningful patterns without checking whether the images produced are correct.

Evaluation of schema theory – weaknesses:

(a) Some of the research experiments, such as Loftus (above) have been criticized for lack of ecological validity. A further follow-up on Loftus' experiment using people who witnessed a real accident (Yuille and Cutshall, 1986) did not show any influence from leading questions (involving 'smashed' 'collided' and 'bumped'). This raises the issue of whether 'reconstructive memory' might be distorted by laboratory conditions, such

as demand characteristics (trying to give the answer that seems most likely to please the interviewer).
(b) Difficulties involved in identifying specific schemas and understanding how and to what degree they interrelate with other schemas.

Overall, it appears that reconstructive memory becomes more inaccurate the further the experience is distanced from the person's existing operating schemas.

Evaluate two models or theories of one cognitive process *(for example memory)* **with reference to research studies**

Cognitive researchers and neuroscientists work together to find out how brain structures are involved in the memory process. Cognitive psychology breaks down the memory process into three separate aspects:

(a) Encoding: entry of information sensed and transformed into the memory system.

(b) Storage: keeping the information in the memory system.

(c) Retrieval: accessing the memory store when the information is needed.

ATKINSON AND SHIFFRIN MULTI-STORE MEMORY MODEL (1968) is a model of cognitive processing and retention of information. It focuses on memory storage and recall being a linear process. The cognitive processes are selective attention, encoding into the memory, and retrieval from the memory.

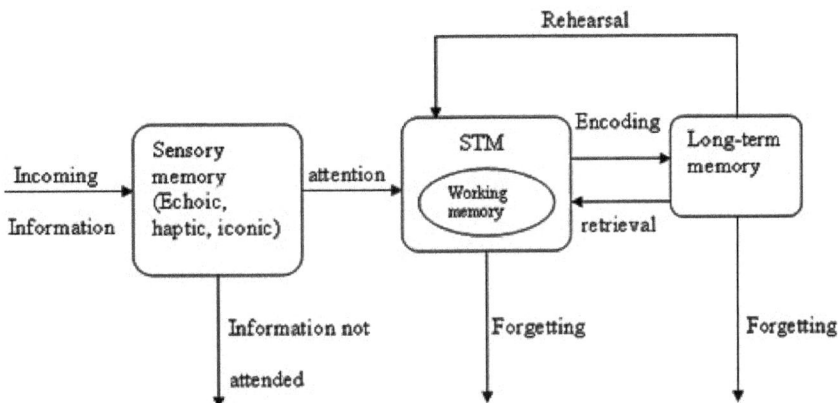

(i) Incoming information not attended-to is lost. That which is attended-to is passed on by the sensory memory. It is then eligible for:

(ii) Coding into the STM (short-term memory; lasts 6-12 seconds). It needs to be rehearsed in order to keep it in, or it can be 'displaced' and lost (Think of your straining to remember a seven-figure telephone number). That may further undergo:

(iii) Coding into LTM (long-term memory) – information may then be lost by interference (e.g. distraction).

In other words, this model regards the memory stores as the structural components of the model. It also proposed control processes, including attention, coding, and rehearsal, that cause items to enter and leave the memory stores.

STRENGTHS OF THE MODEL:

(a) Studies of anterograde amnesia patients (see the case of Clive Wearing below; in an exam you may have to go in to detail) show a good recall of instructions given in the last few seconds (good STM), but very poor recall of those given less recently (poor LTM), suggesting different stores.

(b) In free-recall experiments (e.g. Murdock, 1962) involving memorizing lists of words, subjects tend to remember those that are most likely to have been well-rehearsed (in the beginning, before the novelty of taking part in an experiment has worn off – rehearsal in to LTM), and those at the very end of the list (STM, before forgotten through lack of rehearsal).

WEAKNESSES OF THE MODEL:

(a) Too simple – it does not take into account the different levels and motivations for processing information. It assumes that memory processes are passive. But we more readily succeed in memorizing numbers if they are the digits of people we would like to meet again than if they are mere random numbers.

(b) The ability to visualize and recall the sound of something at the same time strongly indicates that the STM is not one single store.

BADDELEY AND HITCH WORKING MEMORY MODEL (1974), which challenged the multi-store's model short-term memory store. It holds that working memory is an active store, designed to hold and manipulate information that is currently being consciously thought about. **It contains three separate STM components**, each of which operates in parallel at the same time, and all lead to the **LTM**.

(i) The Central Executive: (the selective sensory memory component) is a controlling attention mechanism with a limited capacity. It decides which information is picked up, and passed in to which ones of the three STM systems that work in parallel.

(ii) The three STM subsystems – are two-way systems between the central executive and the LTM. The central executive selectively directs into those three channels (three separate components) visual and conceptually-based information. These can be operating at the same time: you can visualize and think about a concept simultaneously. (You claim that when you tell your teacher that you pay attention while doodling over your notepad.)

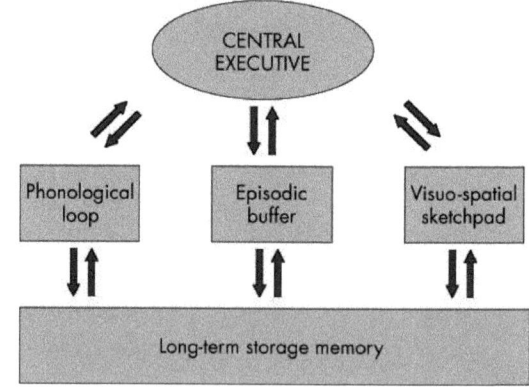

- **The phonological loop** (or 'articulatory loop') as a whole deals with sound or phonological information. It consists of two parts: a **short-term phonological (sound) store** with auditory memory traces that if left alone is quickly lost, but it is supported by an **articulatory rehearsal component** (sometimes called the articulatory loop) that can revive the memory traces. This 'inner voice' repeats the series of words (or other speech elements) on a 'loop' to prevent them from decaying.
- **The visual-spatial sketchpad** - or 'inner eye' which holds visual and spatial information from either the central executive, or returned and activated from the long term memory store.
- **The episodic buffer** is a separate complex memory device enabling you to recall an interrelated set of phenomena, such as a personal story, the sound of your favorite

pop group, or how you felt as you came off your first-ever roller-coaster ride. It is much like a television recall of an event.

(iii) The LTM – which receives from, and releases to the three STM systems above.

STRENGTHS OF MODEL:

(a) In contrast to the multi-store model, this working memory model can accommodate a person's ability to visualize and recall the sound of something at the same time, as it accepts that the STM is not one single store. It explains how people can multi-task.

(b) Problems in studying by one method may be put right through studying by another method. For example, those who have difficulties in following a lecture (phonological loop), can master the material with a different means using a different STM such as a series of diagrams (visual sketchpad). This explains why the lecture method can fail; where a person is a visual learner rather than an auditory learner.

(c) The spread of memory functions into different stores explains many STM deficits shown by brain-damaged patients, as exemplified by the Clive Wearing case below.

WEAKNESSES OF MODEL:

(a) The nature and role of the central executive is still unclear – and with it, the exact way in which the three elements of the STM interrelate.

(b) The need to incorporate the existence of other stores (the episodic buffer was not in the original 1974 model, but added later) by evidence of brain-damaged patients able to recall anecdotes.

Research study on amnesia – how brain damage affects memory processing (a cognitive process).

Amnesia is the inability to learn new information or retrieve information that has already been stored in the memory. **Anterograde amnesia** is the failure to store memories after brain damage. **Retrograde amnesia** is the failure to recall memories that have been stored before brain damage. The brain damage may be caused by brain injury or infection. In behavioral decision-making, this will mean being cut off from past experiences and/or not being able to act with regard to future consequences of the behavior.

The case of H.M. – suffered head injury at age 9 (in 1957), which cause serious epileptic seizures. Doctors removed the tissue from the temporal lobe of the brain (there was no effective drug treatment at the time), including the hippocampus. Following the operation, HM could recall information acquired early in life, but could not form new memories; a case of anterograde amnesia. HM's brain was scanned in 1997, showing that the areas that had been damaged included the hippocampus and amygdala regions. The fact that HM's memory functioned at all indicated that memory functions are more widely distributed throughout the brain than previously thought, and not just in the hippocampus and amygdala regions.

The case of Clive Wearing (current) - in 1985 Clive Wearing, a distinguished middle-aged English musician and musicologist, suffered a brain infection which interfered with memory. It reduced the memory span to a few seconds – practically living in the very present only. His amnesia was mainly anterograde. He could still perform and conduct the music he knew before the infection. His emotional memory prior to the infection was unaffected: he still loved his wife. This indicates that different memory functions are distributed widely throughout the brain.

Evaluation of studies: These findings are supported by recent studies of the brain showing that the hippocampus stores the explicit long term memory (things like facts and figures), and the amygdala tends to hold emotional experiences, but the implicit long-term memory (e.g. how to play the piano) would be located elsewhere in the brain, as illustrated by the Clive Wearing case.

Modern brain scanning procedures showed up exactly which areas were affected by HM's operation (the damage turned out to be widespread), and also made it possible to pinpoint the precise nature of the biological damage to Clive Wearing's brain. These studies have the scope of demonstrating which parts of the brain relate to which aspects of human behavior. However:

- The scanners were not used in the natural environment – issue of ecological validity.
- The information scanners' colored light responses may exaggerate the different activities in the brain.
- The brain areas might light up on the machine for reasons other than those supposed by the investigator.

Explain how biological factors may affect one cognitive process *(for example brain damage)*.

See above on brain damage and how different parts of the brain (biological factors) are responsible for different memory functions. Review case studies of HM and Clive Wearing.

Discuss how social or cultural factors *(for example education)* affect one cognitive process.

Cross-cultural psychologists know that if you wish to test memory in a group of people, it is necessary to have an insight into the language and culture of the group.

This is illustrated by the work of **Cole and Scribner (1974).** This study compared the recall of a series of words in the US, and in the Kpelle people of rural Liberia. The researchers were aware that the words chosen in Liberia were relevant to the environments and lifestyles of the Kpelle people.

The researchers asked Liberian children from different age groups to recall as many items as possible from four categories: utensils, clothes, tools, and vegetables.

It was expected that the older children would score higher, but on investigation that was only true for children attending school. Those who did not attend school did not perform substantially better at age 15 than at age 10. Those who did attend school learnt the lists as rapidly as those children in the US, using the same skills for recalling, which was based on the category-similarity of the objects. Unschooled children did not use *chunking* - grouping bits of information around larger units to help them to remember.

Evaluation – even though all can remember, strategies for memory are not universal. The psychological studies in this field have associations with formal schooling, using a logical structure which is different to those of the unschooled people of the Kpelle tribe. It appears that they learn to remember in ways relevant for their everyday lives, which are not always along the lines that Western-trained cognitive psychologists investigate.

With reference to relevant research studies, to what extent is one cognitive process reliable *(for example, reconstructive memory)*?

See reconstructive memory (above), and the work of Bartlett, and Loftus and Palmer. They suggest that reconstructive memory becomes more inaccurate the further the experience is distanced from the person's existing operating schemas.

Discuss the use of technology in investigating cognitive processes *(for example, MRI scans in memory research, fMRI scans in decision-making research)*.

PET (positron emission tomography) SCANS IN MEASURING ALZHEIMER'S DISEASE-ASSOCIATED MEMORY LOSS BEHAVIOR

This scanning method can record functions in different parts of the brain, such as the way it metabolizes glucose, and the blood flow. Reduced metabolism of glucose in the hippocampus part of the brain can indicate the onset of Alzheimer's disease and its associated deterioration of the cognitive process of memory. This is demonstrated by memory loss and difficulties in recognizing people and objects.

The study of **Mosconi et al (2005),** showed that in a longitudinal study (where participants are followed up at intervals over a period of time) of some 50 patients who started out as normal and healthy, those who showed early signs of reduced metabolism in the hippocampus were associated with later developments in Alzheimer's disease. It appears that PET scans could be useful in the very early detection of Alzheimer's disease and its behavior associated with lack of memory processing – a cognitive function in decline.

MRI and fMRI give a three-dimensional image of brains structures, and at the same time have the capacity to record changes in the use of oxygen in the blood. When the brain is more active, it uses more oxygen. Thus it can show when your brain is active in a task such as reading, or even in promoting market research, such as detecting which parts are active and the degree of brain activity when your favorite brand fills the screen. This is exemplified in the study of **Kilts (2003),** to investigate the role of the brain in product preferences – neuro-marketing. The self-selected sample of volunteers were first required to rate the given list of consumer goods in order of preference, assigning points to the degree of attractiveness. Then they were attached to an MRI scanner, where they were shown pictures of the same items and asked to rate them again, according to attractiveness. The study found that every time a person rated a product as very attractive, there was increased activity in the medial prefrontal cortex of the brain – the area found to be related to our sense of self and our personality. Thus this feeling of 'excitement' shown up in the brain is what affects the decision-making process when weighing up: 'to buy or not to buy'.

Evaluation – it seems that it is possible to use knowledge of neuro-marketing to test the efficiency of marketing methods, and different brands. The dream of any company is to link the product with the person's sense of self (e.g. are you a Nike man?). However, this does raise ethical issues: should marketing firms and political consultants be able to look inside the brain, they could deduce exactly how to manipulate the cognitive schemas of society to their continuing profits.

In addition:
- The scanners are not used in natural environments for cognition – raising the issue of ecological validity.
- The information they send in the form of colors may exaggerate the different activities in the brain.

- The brain areas might light up on the machine for different reasons than those supposed by the investigator.

B. Cognition and Emotion

To what extent do cognitive and biological factors interact in emotion *(for example, the shorter and longer path of emotion in the brain)*?

Emotions are a combination of biological and cognitive factors. They involve:

(a) Physiological changes – involuntary arousing the autonomic nervous system and endocrine system.

(b) Your own feeling of an emotion – e.g. anger, surprise, happiness.

(c) Associated behavior – such a smiling or running away.

There are two paths of emotion in the brain (following LeDoux's model, 1999). When the brain is stimulated (for example, you are extremely annoyed), your grasp of the situation (i.e. the cognitive process) goes simultaneously along two routes – the short route and the long route. The short route gives an animal-type response and is immediate. It goes from the sensory thalamus (pick-up point of cognition) directly to the amygdala, which dictates the action. There is no rationalization. At the same time, the information is processed in more depth and in a more rational manner through the long, more complex route. That goes from the sensory thalamus via the sensory cortex and hippocampus to the amygdala. It takes several seconds, but this process works through the issue before responding. That is the reason it is a good idea to count to ten before losing your temper…

Link between cognitive and biological factors – the biological elements show two simultaneous processes of cognition. The short route brings less complex schemas into cognitive processing, but is vital in emergencies as it saves the time that could be a matter of life and death. The long route brings more complex schemas into play and allows for a more reasonable and intelligent interpretation of a situation, which can help people to avoid inappropriate responses to situations.

Evaluate one theory of how emotion may affect one cognitive process *(for example, flashbulb memory)*

Flashbulb memory is a special type of emotional memory which relates to specific events. It not only recalls the event, but brings up the emotions that went with the event (the whole thing is incorporated as with a flash picture on a camera). This concept, put forward by **Brown and Kulik (1977)** found that those interviewed said that they had very clear memories of where they were, what they did, and what they felt when they first heard the news of the death of J. F. Kennedy, and Martin Luther King.

They suggest that there may be a specialized neural mechanism which sets off an emotional arousal because of the very deep impression made by the event. Indeed, emotional events are better remembered than less emotional events because of the crucial role of the emotional part of the brain – the amygdala. In other words, the emotions and events are registered in the same 'flashbulb memory package' and a recollection of the event recalls your personal situations surrounding it and the way you felt.

In evaluation, Brown and Kulik seem to have identified two important determinants of the 'flashbulb memory package' – event importance, and event emotionality.

However, flashbulb memory has been questioned by the work of Neisser and Harsch (1992). They argue that flashbulb memory may be a narrative – where people take later events and put them back into the memory, mixing them with 'flashbulb event'. It may be that there is still a special memory mechanism for the 'flashbulb memory package', but if there is, does the memory last any longer than 'normal' memories? Indeed, Neisser and Harsch's investigation followed the 1986 space shuttle disaster indicated that some 40% of the participants who recalled the event showed distinct memory distortion, which they argued was based on information found out sometime after the event that was being fed into the memory of the actual event. In addition, the studies of flashbulb memories are non-experimental: they do not include control conditions that distinguish between 'normal' memories and flashbulb memories.

POSSIBLE EXAMINATION QUESTIONS

SHORT ANSWER QUESTIONS

Outline two methods that may be used at the cognitive level of analysis.

Explain how one social or cultural factor may affect one cognitive process.

LONG ANSWER QUESTIONS

Evaluate two models or theories of one cognitive process with reference to research studies.

Evaluate schema theory with reference to two research studies.

CHAPTER THREE - THE SOCIO-CULTURAL LEVEL OF ANALYSIS

Paper 1 – core topic

Socio-cultural psychology recognizes that the behavior of the individual may be better understood when the social and cultural contexts are taken into account. **The socio-cultural perspective emphasizes how the presence and behavior of one or a few people affect the behavior and attitudes of another individual.** It also provides a broader framework for exploring topics such as aggression, which is often regarded as an individual personality trait.

As social psychologists continue to integrate the biological and cultural contributions into social behavior, there is a general consensus that a synthesis of the biological, cognitive and sociocultural levels of psychological analysis brings us closer to understanding the complex interacting systems that make up the human being.

Socio-cultural psychologist work on premises including the following:

1. *Our social and cultural environment influences our behavior* – for example, eleven-year-old students know exactly how to handle the classroom routines of speaking to the teacher in the correct mode, interacting appropriately with a group of other students when working together, and handling conflicts in the classroom and the playground. Such a child entering the classroom for the first time after being homeschooled may be completely 'lost'. He/she could suffer months of painful adjustment for having gone without the social and cultural aspects of conventional schooling. (The same principle can apply to those switching schools – where the social norms of the previous schools are quite different to the new one.) This would involve issues of *conformity* (see Asch, below, and *compliance* (Lynn and McCall, below)

2. *We want to feel connected with other people, and we want to identify with groups of people.* That can mean going through persistent and tough qualifying to be accepted by the group of your choice, whether in dress or deed. It can mean having one's judgment swayed by majority influence (see Asch, below – make sure you understand how that study's research illustrates this point), or a particularly influential minority (see Moscovici, below).

3. *People have a social self* – for example, if your football team wins you see yourself as part of the victory as you go out to celebrate: "We won the cup!" Even if you can't kick a football in the right direction. The dynamics of social identity, with resulting group conflict, prejudice, and discrimination are exemplified in the 'Robber's Cave' study by Sherif, below.

In an exam, expand these studies where relevant.

METHODS USED AT THE SOCIO-CULTURAL LEVEL OF ANALYSIS INCLUDE:

1. Laboratory experiments - exemplified by Bandura's study on social learning theory (1965, see below). This involved test and control samples to determine the acceptance or rejection of a hypothesis. The conditions are the same except that the IV (independent variable – in that case witnessing the adult beating up the Bobo doll) is applied to the test sample only. This also used non-participant observation, to gauge the children's behavior under the stress.

2. Participant observation – exemplified by the work of Festinger (1956). This studied the way of life of a group which believed that the world was coming to an end on December 31st of that year. Those following the group's rituals, texts and ideologies would rescued by a flying saucer. Observation may be participant observation as in this study, where the researcher becomes involved in the everyday life of those being observed, or non-participant. It may be overt (with the group's knowledge) or covert (without the group's knowledge).

3. Content analysis: exemplified Hofstede's classic study (1973, see below). That involved studying the morale in the IBM workplace, a multi-national company employing people of many nations and cultures. Hofstede carried out a content analysis of the responses (see chapter 9 under 'content analysis') received from the 40 most represented countries in the survey. The trends were analyzed, used a source of grounded theory (inductive content analysis – see chapter 9), and presented as cultural dimensions.

In an exam, expand these studies where relevant.

ETHICAL CONSIDERATIONS: similar to those in the biological and cognitive approach, including:

1. Informed consent – participants must know the object of the study, that their involvement is voluntary, what the data will be used for, and if necessary be debriefed at the end of the study. In extreme cases, the ethical requirement for informed consent might be waived, when the focus of the study is of public importance and there is no other way to obtain the information.

2. Making the participants anonymous to protect them, even at the risk of reducing the authenticity of the research and of preventing any follow-up study.

3. Bearing in mind that socio-cultural research is an extremely sensitive issue with many ethnic groups. Typically, the elders of the society must be consulted for permission to work with members of their group.

A. Sociocultural cognition

Socio-cultural cognition may be defined as how we understand and think about people and social situations.

People do not passively observe the behavior of others, but they try to explain it. Andrew arrives ten minutes late to the first class of the day. The teacher explodes with 'time waits for no-one'. He proceeds to waste the next ten minutes lecturing on the anti-social practice of unpunctuality instead of getting on with the lesson. The boy's cognitive schemas just cannot make sense of the situation. Is it because the teacher hates him? Is it because he is obsessed with punctuality? Is it because he missed breakfast? Is it because he's overtired and in a bad mood?

Describe the role of situational and dispositional factors in explaining behavior.

Attribution theory is how people interpret and explain causal relationships and things that happen in the social world.

In other words, people are acting as naïve psychologists. Situational and dispositional factors are frameworks used by people to understand and come to terms with the other's behavior.

Situational means that what happened was nothing to do with them – no reflection on them. Dispositional is that it had everything to do with them. The teacher's disproportionate reactions to Andrew might be dispositional (he has been waiting to 'get at' Andrew), or situational (he just wanted a straight lesson with no interruptions, and Andrew happened to 'get in the way'). Jill has spent two hours getting ready for a date. She gets to the restaurant right on time, at 8pm. It is already 8:25. The rain is crashing down, and Jack still hasn't turned up. That growing unpleasant feeling gnaws away at the pit of her tummy. What's happened? Is it because he doesn't care, or likes to show her that 'he's boss' (dispositional), or is it because his usual bus got cancelled and there was a long wait for another – perhaps due to the rain (situational)? And that the deluge put his cellphone out of action?

The study of Morris and Peng (1994) suggests that situational and dispositional factors in explaining behavior may be influenced by culture. Their participants were American and Chinese students currently studying in the United States. Students drawn from both nationalities were presented with accounts of two recent murder events. The first murderer was a Chinese student who did not get the scholastic appointment that he wanted at a leading American university. The second murderer was an employee (a postman) who shot his boss. Both murderers committed suicide soon afterwards.

For each case, participants were required to rate the likelihood of various explanations for pulling the trigger. The researchers supplied a list of situational and dispositional causes. The results showed that the American students rated the dispositional factors as the most important, such as believing that murder was the way to redress grievance. In contrast, the Chinese emphasized the situational, such as the murderer being under very high social pressure to climb the academic ladder. Whether the actual murder had been committed by an American or a Chinese was immaterial in attributing the cause of the murder.

Discuss two errors in attributions

(a) Attribution error #1 - Fundamental attribution error (FAE) – when people overestimate the role of dispositional factors and underestimate the role of situational factors, or the other way round. For example, people who are excellent public speakers or are in high positions are often given credit for being much cleverer than they really are.

This is shown by the study of **Lee et al. (1977)**. Participating university students were randomly allocated to the role of game-show host, game-show contestant, or spectator. The questions were put together by the game-show host. The spectators watched the entire show. Afterwards, they were given the job of rating the intelligence of the participants.

The result: the game-show host was consistently believed to be cleverest! His was the only situation that gave the chance to display stand-up wit and magnetic personality.

This can explain why people who are proficient in one field are often wrongly attributed to having expertise in other fields. For example, doctors are frequently consulted by their patients on non-medical matters.

The study may be criticized as it was carried out on exclusively university students who were used to looking up to those in 'professor-type' roles. Indeed, it put the game show host in a framework where he was motivated to 'play to the gallery'. He was the one person who had the freedom to activate and display his charisma and indeed intelligence to full effect.

(b) Attribution error #2 - Self-serving bias error (SSB) – when people interpret events and situations according to their own feelings and agendas. You get a top grade in IB psychology: 'I'm a great psychologist'. You do badly: 'It's all the teacher's fault'.

SSB is where people take credit for their successes, attributing them to dispositional factors rather than situational factors. And they disassociate themselves from their failures, putting them down to situational factors. We use SSB as a means of psychological protection; to protect our self-esteem.

The reverse appears in certain non-Western cultures. The cross-cultural study of **Kashima and Triandis (1986)** showed that there were significant cultural differences between North American and Japanese students. Each participant viewed a series of picture slides. They were then tested on their recall of the details of the scenes on the slides. In commenting on their performance, the North Americans focused on their success. They attributed it to their good memory recall. The Japanese, on the other hand, focused on what they did not remember. They thought in terms of having to improve their memory skills. Thus the North Americans viewed their scores through a self-serving bias, and the Japanese through an anti-self-serving bias, a modesty bias.

Kashima and Triandis suggested that the modesty bias was a reflection of the collective nature of Japanese society. The North American SSB, on the other hand, typified the individual achievement-based character of Western society

Evaluate social identity theory, making reference to relevant studies.

Social identity theory is where people strive to improve their self-image through personal achievement, and/or being accepted in groups which express their ideals, identity, and dreams. If you are 'in' with the group you choose to be part of, you develop the image of that group. For example, if you aspire to be the "cool rebel without a cause" you might grab the back seat of the bus, together with the other troublemakers.

The work of Tajfel et al (1971) involved the random assignment of boys to two different groups on one criterion only; artwork of Kandinsky or Klee – which is preferred? The results were that those in each group showed in-group favoritism, believing that their group was the better one, without actually showing any active dislike for the other one.

Active dislike of the other group has been only shown to thrive where there is competition – demonstrated by the 'Robber's Cave' experiment conducted by Sherif (1954). He wanted to understand the dynamics of social identity, group conflict, prejudice, and discrimination. He selected a group of 22 white 11 year-old boys who were unknown to each other. They were taken to a remote summer camp in Robber's Cave State Park in Oklahoma, USA, randomly put in to two groups, neither knowing of the existence of the other. The first week was dedicated to team-building activities – hiking and swimming together. Each group chose a name for itself – Eagles and Rattlers, with those names on their shirts and flags.

Then they were introduced to each other though a series of competitions, with prizes for the winners and nothing for the losers. Tensions rose between them, demonstrating their prejudices and showing discriminatory behavior: derogatory songs on the other, burning each other's flag, and refusing to eat together with the other group.

Following was the integration phase. The two groups watched movies together. The hope was that these face-to-face encounters would reduce tensions. But meetings broke up with the two groups throwing food at each other.

Finally, the researchers arranged situations in which a problem arose which threatened both groups at the same time. It included a blockage of the supply of drinking water to the camp. The two groups managed to work together to remove it, and celebrated when they succeeded. By the time these trials were over, they stopped having negative images of the other side. On the final bus-ride home, the members of one team used their prize money to buy drinks for everyone.

The conclusions of Sherif were: (a) that competition over scarce resources is a vital element in the active dislike of another group (b) the need to combine together to defeat the common threat creates a bond between two competing different groups. And in turn, to wipe out the negative stereotypes one group has of the other.

Evaluation: social identity theory appears to contribute to our understanding on how people seek to improve their self-esteems through striving to take on a personally-desired social identity. Social identity theory highlights how our fundamental need to be part of the society we choose can influence our behavior. However, its limitations include: failing to explain why in some situations personal principles are stronger than identification with the group (e.g. keeping off the alcohol where heavy drinking is the group norm), and that practical motivators such as poverty and the rewards expected for being in the group are more important determinants of behavior than group identity (for example, identification and involvement with the drug-pushing culture).

Explain the formation of stereotypes and their effect on behavior.

Stereotyping involves categorizing a person based on his/her visible cues, such as gender, nationality, race, religion etc. It assumes that all members of the group have the characteristics attributed to the group. An individual is thought to have the characteristics believed to be the norm of the group he is part of (e.g. Americans are rich, the Germans are precise). It can be positive or negative: 'women are bad drivers' or 'women are good speakers'. The stereotype could well be an illusion – for example nearly half the USA's families are classified as low-income or below the poverty line, and less than one percent have bank balances exceeding $1 million.

Indeed, stereotypes assign similar characteristics to all members of a group, despite the reality that group members may vary widely from one another.

The formation of stereotypes is argued to be a social-learning phenomenon, coming from personal experience with other people, mentor figures, and the media. The stereotype can be developed from direct experience with one member of the group. This may be reinforced by **confirmation bias** (Snyder and Swan, 1978). That means that people will subsequently confirm their stereotypes by focusing on experiences that confirm the stereotype, and ignore those which contradict the stereotype, regarding the latter as exceptions to the rule. There will appear to an **illusory correlation** - a relationship between two elements where there is not. For example a woman fined for going through a red light will confirm the 'bad driver' stereotype. A young man caught doing the same thing will be "too much testosterone behind the wheel". (Attribution errors may be a result of confirmation bias.)

The formation of stereotypes is also argued to be a socio-cognitive phenomenon, based on schemas. Social cognition is based on **social representations:** the shared beliefs (right or wrong) of the society we belong to. These representations combine into a personal schema which is applied to classify the various aspects of peoples and cultures worldwide (Moscovici, 1973). These schemas enable the simplifying of a very complex reality, when we are put in an unfamiliar situation (for example a vacation in a country whose language we do not speak) with too much information to process comfortably.

The work of Cohen (1981) involved the showing of a video of a woman having dinner with her husband. Half the participants were told that she was a waitress, the other half that she was a librarian. They were asked to recall the video. The waitress group tended to emphasize the parts of the video that confirmed that role (e.g. beer drinking). The other group did the same for the librarian stereotype (e.g. spectacles, classical music in the background). This study emphasized that we are likely to remember information fitting in with our cognitive schemas of how people in given roles are expected to look and behave.

Effect on behavior: bias occurs when the stereotype is positively activated, prejudice when the stereotype is negatively activated.

Stereotyping and resulting prejudice (=attitude) and discrimination (=negative behavior resulting from prejudices) may be rooted in competition for scarce resources, causing aggressive behavior: *See the Sherif study above, on prejudice and discrimination.*

Stereotyping may cause the feelings of suffering discrimination and resulting spotlight anxiety. The work of Spencer et al. (1977) tested the effect of stereotype threat on intellectual performance. The researchers gave a difficult mathematics test to students who were established as being strong in that subject. They hypothesized that the women (being under the common stereotype of women not being good at maths) would underperform compared to the men taking the test. They did underperform – significantly. When those researchers subsequently tested their skills in literature, the two groups performed equally well. The conclusions were that women did not suffer undue anxiety, as women are not stereotype-threatened in literature.

Stereotypes can be activated automatically and influence behavior, as illustrated by **the work of Bargh et al (1996)**. Participants were in the framework of a language-proficiency test. They were given lists of words and had to put them into sentences. Some were given words that were related to the senior citizen stereotype: (e.g. retired, grey, wise). Others were given words that were unrelated to the stereotype (e.g. clean, thirsty, private). On completion of the exercise, participants were told to make their way to the elevator. Unknown to them, they were being observed and timed (covert observation). Those whose senior citizen stereotype had been activated walked somewhat more slowly to the elevator than those who whose senior citizen stereotype had not been activated.

B. Social norms

Explain social learning theory, making reference to two relevant studies.

SOCIAL LEARNING THEORY – MODELLING – suggests that much behavior, including aggression, is **learnt** from the environment and the process of **modeling.** Modeling involves learning through **observation** of other people (models), which may lead to **imitation** if the behavior to be copied appears to lead to desirable consequences.

Be aware that social learning theory may be used to explain aspects of stereotyping, as people model the attitudes and reactions of others.

It involves paying attention to the person modeled, remembering the behavior that was observed, subsequently replicating the action, and feeling good about demonstrating what has been learnt. It is distinguished from conditioning, in that the learning is indirect (not stimulus/response/reward). It models the behavior of others (vicarious learning), and gets indirect reinforcement (vicarious reinforcement) according to the results of following that behavior.

For example, many believed that the human being could not run a four-minute mile before Roger Bannister succeeded in 1954. Within the next few months that record had been broken several times as leading athletes had learnt by his example that it could be done.

Models may be categorized under two headings: **positional models** (e.g. cartoon figures, famous people) and **personal models** (role models – parents, teachers, peers, and community leaders). The latter models are more likely to be sources of long-term developments of social behavior.

Bandura's (1965) study in social learning theory aimed to demonstrate that learning can occur through mere observation of a model, and that imitation can take place in the absence of the model.

His team investigated whether children would imitate the aggression modeled by an adult, and also whether children were more likely to imitate same-gender models.

Method – 36 boys and 36 girls aged 3-6 were divided into similar groups, Group 1 was exposed to adult models who showed aggression by bashing an inflatable 'Bobo' doll. Group 2 observed a non-aggressive adult who assembled toys for 10 minutes. Group 3 was the control and did not see any model. In groups 1 and 2, some watched same-sex models and others watched opposite-sex models. All groups were then placed in a room with toys. As they were 'getting in' to the toys, they were removed and told that they were for other children (this was the provocation to possible aggression). They were then left with the Bobo doll.

Results – those exposed to aggression at the earlier stage showed significantly more aggression towards the Bobo doll than those who had not been exposed to aggression. The conclusion was that aggression is learnt; it is not part of the child's nature. Also, boys were more likely to imitate the physical aggression they had seen from men, and the girls were more likely to imitate the verbal aggression they had seen from women.

Evaluation: the study does appear to support social learning theory, i.e. that we copy the behavior learnt from others. Indeed, the models did perform aggressive acts that were not likely to be within the children's repertoires.

However, it was in a laboratory setting; low ecological validity. The children may well have not related beating a doll which bounced back with a smile to actual aggression. Also they were likely to be frustrated when the toys were taken away – whether they witnessed the aggressive scenes or not. There was a very brief encounter with the model, which contrasted to the long hours children view aggressive scenes on television. There was no follow-up study to assess how long-lasting the violence learning-experience was. Finally, the issue of demand characteristics – the children might have acted aggressively in order to please the researchers.

By today's ethical standards, there would be the issue of the merits of provoking very young children and exposing them to violence for research purposes.

This contrasts with the St Helena study (Charlton et al. 2002) – based on observing the degree of violence in the school playground environment before and after the introduction of television on that island in 1995. A content analysis of TV programs showed a similar level of violence as TV in the UK. However, the observations showed no significant change in the pre-television-day low degree of violence after the introduction of TV on St. Helena. This study therefore downplays the importance of social learning theory.

Unlike Bandura, the study took place in the ecological-valid school playground setup, by covert observations. It may be criticized as pre-1995 St. Helena children might have experienced violent-behavior learning experiences from media other than television (books, comics, movies) which might have served the same function as television in the UK, and were in a cultural environment which was less inclined to tolerate similar conduct.

It may also be argued that the television-based violent characters in the St. Helena study were positional models. They were less likely to be models of violence for children, as they were personally unknown them, and for much part were not close to them. In contrast, the very young children in Bandura - who saw and trusted the researchers as associates of their parent/school environment - might well have viewed the researchers as personal models, as extensions of their parents and teachers. Consequently, the children identified more closely with the researcher, and would have more readily modeled the violent behavior.

Gergely et. al's (2002) study in social learning theory demonstrated that under certain conditions humans will carry out a task by sub-optimal means as a result of social learning. This study incorporated two groups of 14-month-old infants, and a box that would light up with a simple push. The first group watched the demonstrator light up the box by pressing the box with her bent-over forehead. Her hands were free. The second group also saw the box being lit up by head-pressure, but the demonstrator's hands were busy arranging a blanket around her shoulders.

The infants then operated the light-box for themselves. Two thirds of the infants in the first group used their heads. Less than a quarter in the second group used their heads.

The findings of this study appear to highlight the notion that one year-old infants can engage successfully in quite sophisticated social learning. The different results of the two groups indicate that social learning is not a simple reflex, mirror-imaging process. They suggest that there is a dimension of individual reasoning involved. The first group accepted that the box lit up though an unexpected movement, as that is what they saw the demonstrator do. They assumed that head-pressure was crucial to the process. The second group observed the same method, but associated it with the demonstrator's hands being otherwise engaged. Therefore three-quarters operated the box with their hands, rather than with their heads.

Evaluation: the study does appear to support social learning theory, i.e. that we copy the behavior learnt from others. As in Bandura, the model did perform acts that were not likely to be within the infants' repertoires. It also indicates that we select the behavior that we wish to copy, as being crucial to our own interests.

But as in Bandura, the encounter with the box and the demonstrator was brief. It was not clear how much learning actually took place in the first group: would a follow-up study a few months later show as many as two-thirds continuing to operate the same box with their heads? Also, their interest in getting the light to work at that moment might have made them comply with the demonstrator's method. Like Bandura, the demonstrator's role could be argued as being positional rather than personal.

Discuss the use of compliance techniques *(for example, lowballing, foot-in-the-door, reciprocity)*.

Compliance is where a person carries out a request to do something under direct pressure, even though the pressure may not necessarily be perceived by that person (e.g. in advertising). This contrasts with **conformity,** which is where the situation does not use direct pressure, but pressure is often perceived by individuals as influencing their behavior. **Compliance techniques include:**

(a) Reciprocity – people comply out of feeling that they need to return a favor. People feel they must repay what another person has provided. For example Lynn and McCall (1998) found that restaurant diners leave a bigger tip when the bill comes together with a candy.

(b) Door-in-the-face technique – make a request which is turned down, because it is obviously too big. Then make a second smaller request, which might well be accepted – as the person will feel that the request has been reduced to accommodate them. Cialdini (1975) and his team tried to persuade one group of university students to chaperone a group of juvenile delinquents on a trip to the zoo. Nearly all refused. Then the same people stopped another group of students and firstly asked them if they would sign on as volunteer counselors for two hours weekly for two years. They said no. Then afterwards, they asked them to chaperone a same day trip to the zoo. Half said yes.

(c) Foot-in-the-door technique – for example the study of Dickerson (1992), where the team wanted students to conserve water by taking shorter showers (in Santa Cruz, California, where water is in short supply). To do so, they asked students to sign a poster that said: "Take shorter showers. If I can do it, so can you." (That was the foot in the door.) Then later on, they asked them to time the period they took for a shower. Overall, it turned out to be much shorter than the average time for students as a whole.

(d) Low-balling – for example the study of Cialdini (1974) on a group of enthusiastic first-year university psychology students. The first group of enthusiasts was asked to take part in a study on cognition and that they were to be there at 7:00 a.m. Less than one quarter agreed. In the second group, they were asked the same thing, but not told a time. More than half agreed to take part. When the 7:00 a.m. time was revealed, nearly all turned up on time.

(e) Hazing – involves a series of initiation rites required to join a group perceived as exclusive, such as a college fraternity or sorority. In deciding to join, the individual complies with the often dramatic and stringent ceremonies. This initial degree of compliance leads to a greater degree of compliance later on, within the group activities. The study of Aronson and Mills (1959) involved asking female students to join a sex discussion-group. They were placed into two groups. The first had to go through an embarrassing initiation procedure to join. The second was allowed in straight away. Once both groups were in the meeting, the activity involved accomplices who were instructed to conduct an extremely boring program. Those who went through the initiation commented on the meeting being valuable and instructive. Those who were admitted straight away found the meeting to be a waste of time. Thus early compliance demanding initial sacrifices appears to lead to a greater commitment to comply subsequently.

Evaluate research on conformity to group norms.

Conformity is where individuals adjust their behavior to what they perceive is expected of them in a particular situation.

ASCH'S STUDY OF MAJORITY CONFORMITY (1951) (known as the Asch paradigm)

The study aimed to determine whether participants would **conform to majority influence,** which promoted the giving of incorrect answers in a situation where the correct answers were clearly evident.

Each target participant entered a room where there were six other participants, dressed formally in business suits. Participants were told that they were going to take part in "a psychological experiment on visual judgment." Unknown to the target participant, the six others were accomplices of the experimenter.

All participants went through a series of exercises, involving a series of single lines on individual cards, and three comparison lines of different lengths on a second card. Participants had to say, in turn and out loud, which line on the second cards was the same as the one on the first cards. The target participant was placed towards the end of the group.

Accomplices, dressed formally in businesses suits, gave the same wrong answers on 12 of the 18 trials.

Participants conformed to the unanimous majority on a third of the critical trials. Nearly three quarters conformed at least once, but just over one quarter never conformed. In follow-up, some conforming participants claimed to have seen the same as the majority. Others conformed because they did not want to be ridiculed by the group. The majority who conformed did so because they thought that their perception of the lines must be inaccurate, and the majority's accurate.

Thus it seems that even in unambiguous situations, there is still pressure to conform to a unanimous majority. Asch concluded that some people experience social influence and conform to avoid rejection. Others experience informational influence and conform because they doubt their own judgments. Follow-up experiments indicated that a majority of three with no accomplice dissenters was more effective in producing conformity than a majority of eight with one accomplice dissenter.

Evaluation

- The formal and serious atmosphere confronting the target participants did seem to have created an environment where conformity was expected.
- The time and the place that the research was carried out might have affected the findings. In the 1950s, the USA was very conservative and in the grip of McCarthyism, an anti-communist witch-hunt. That placed greater pressure on people to conform, and not 'rock the boat'.
- The work of Perrin and Spenser (1981) led to the conclusion that cultural change over 30 years in the USA led to a reduction in the tendency of students to conform. The study repeated the Asch experiment using mathematics, science, and engineering students as target participants. Only one out of the nearly 400 tested conformed. The researchers concluded that the Asch paradigm was far less significant in American society in the 1980s, which took questioning of 'authority figures' for granted. (It may be argued that the students in the above disciplines were less likely to let themselves be deceived.)
- Bond and Smith (1996) concluded from a meta-analysis of over 100 studies that conformity was more evident in collectivist cultures (valuing group loyalty) than in individualist cultures (valuing individual initiative). People would be more likely to conform in Fiji, Hong-Kong, and Brazil, that in North America and Western Europe.
- Ethical considerations: the original Asch experiment would, by today's standards, have raised the issue of the participants being deceived and made to feel anxious about their performances.

MOSCOVICI ET AL'S STUDY OF MINORITY CONFORMITY (1969)

MINORITY INFLUENCE is a form of social influence where **a persuasive minority group exerts pressure to change the attitudes or behaviors of the majority.**

The study sought to determine whether or not a consistent minority of participants could influence a majority in a color perception task.

172 participants were used. All had good eyesight. Six participants at a time were required to estimate the color of 36 slides. All the slides were blue, but of differing levels of brightness. Two of the six participants were accomplices of the experimenter. There were two situations: consistency (the two accomplices called the slides green on all trials) and inconsistency (the two accomplices called the slides green 24 times and blue 12 times).

Participants in the consistent condition yielded and called the slides green in just over a quarter of the trials. 32% of the participants reported a green slide at least once. Participants in the inconsistent condition called the slides green in just over 1% of the trials. [Also in a later study by Moscovici and Nemeth (1974), it was found that seating position can affect minority influence. If an accomplice (i.e. the minority) was assigned a seat, the seating position was unimportant. But where he chose to sit at the head of the table, he was more influential.]

The study concluded that it is important for a minority to behave consistently over time if they are to influence a majority to change its viewpoint. Individual members of the group must be consistent, and there must be agreement among different members of the minority. Inconsistent minorities lack any real influence on majorities. Their opinions are viewed as groundless.

STRENGTHS

- **The work of Maass and Clark (1984)** found that indeed strong minority influence could influence public opinion, as in Moscovici. That study highlighted two levels of opinion, public and private, over the issue of gay rights. The participants (all heterosexual) attended a debate where different viewpoints were argued. They outwardly related to the majority stance from the heterosexuals, rather than to the homosexuals who were in a minority. Thus publicly expressed views on gay rights supported the majority opinion, but privately the participants expressed viewpoints that shifted towards the minority opinion. That indicated that minorities are more likely to change private opinion before a change in public behavior.

- The consistent nature of the minority influence was maintained in the test situation where the two minority accomplices strongly insisted that the slides were green when they were in fact blue.

WEAKNESSES

- The artificiality of the laboratory setting in the experiment
- The perceived relatively unimportant nature of the task
- Lack of similarity to real-life situations where minorities, such as pressure groups, attempt to exert their influence over the feelings of majority groups

RELEVANCY OF CONFORMITY RESEARCH ON MAJORITY INFLUENCE: Nemeth (2003) claims that people holding minority viewpoints are not just passive recipients of influence. They can sometimes promote a differing viewpoint which is sometimes accepted. We can also profit from minority views – even when they are wrong: exposure to dissenting minority views stimulates people to be better decision makers and also more creative in their thoughts.

Note that throughout the twentieth century, there have been several examples of strong minority commitments which eventually persuaded the majority, including movements for civil rights, and for sustainable environments

Discuss factors influencing conformity *(for example, culture, groupthink, minority influence).*

MINORITY INFLUENCE (see above)

GROUPTHINK – minority opinions are essential in a group's decision-making process, otherwise the group will experience groupthink. Groupthink is where the group has a unanimous (non-disputed) opinion on an issue, and is convinced that its decisions will be accepted. The group decision-making setting is typical in a high-stress situation where there is urgency in reaching a consensus-based decision, within a group that perceives itself to be important and of unchallengeable authority. The high stress reality can mean that members of the group will doubt their own reservations and refrain from voicing any dissenting opinions. This is not the time to 'throw a spanner in the works'. Thus groupthink does not lead to good decision-making.

For example, a group of history students are studying together the causes of World War I, and one student comes up with a historically inaccurate, but plausible explanation. The other students place their faith in that student, rather than verifying his work through outside sources, or brainstorm alternative explanations. The teacher will see the result as several students will have the same imperfect response to the exam question.

The study of Esser and Lindoerfer (1989) examined the evidence and analysis presented by the members of the official commission of inquiry on the space shuttle 'Challenger', which exploded 73 seconds after launch. They found evidence of the stress-ridden atmosphere of the investigation, and detected the groupthink symptoms of the illusions of invulnerability, unanimity, and pressure on dissenters to conform.

CULTURAL ISSUES AND INFLUENCES (see below: conformity is likely to arise in collective rather than individualist cultures, and within cultures that are anxious to avoid uncertainty)

C. Cultural norms

Define the terms 'culture' and 'cultural norms'.

Culture in psychological terms has been defined by Hofstede (2002) as the mental software common to the members of the socio-cultural group.

These cultural schemas have been internalized, so they influence thinking, emotions, and behavior. It is learned through daily interactions and from feedback by members of the same group.

Kuschel (2004) argues that we see the manifestations of culture in behavior. Thus in order to apply culture to psychology, it is necessary to find how specific factors in culture relate to behaviors such as initiation rites, witch doctors, infanticides (killing babies in specific circumstances), and honor-killings.

These factors reflect the ways that these people have survived in their environment, how they have organized life in social groups, and the resulting beliefs, attitudes, and norms which shape their specific behaviors.

Cultural norms are behavior patterns that are typical of specific groups. They are passed down from generation to generation by observational (and reinforcement) learning by the group's 'gatekeepers' (guardians of culture) – parents, teachers, religious leaders, and peers. Cultural norms include such things as how marriage partners are chosen, attitudes towards the rights of animals, spanking children, and alcohol consumption.

(*Use examples from your own culture and/or those you know to develop and illustrate this point*)

Examine the role of two cultural dimensions on behavior *(for example, individualism/collectivism, uncertainty avoidance).*

Cultural dimensions are the issues and perspectives of a culture based on values and cultural norms. For example, doing business in the Middle East means that the deal is drawn out. There is no opening with a focused business meeting, signing of contracts and concluding handshakes. Instead, there are family photos and home hospitality thrown in long before getting down to finalizing the deal. And in the Middle East, the handshake is often the opening of the 'serious' stage of the business deal, not the conclusion of it. In addition, the degree of personal space versus closeness is an issue. British tend to keep a slightly greater personal space from one-another than North Americans; both cultures tend to keep a further distance from each other than in sub-Saharan African and Central Asia.

Hofstede's classic study (1973) focused on the morale in the IBM workplace, a multi-national company employing people of many nations and cultures. He then carried out a content analysis of the responses received from the 40 most represented countries in the survey. The trends were analyzed, and presented as cultural dimensions.

Thus the study of cultural dimensions is vital for cross-cultural communications in international diplomacy, business, and tourism. Our studies focus on the dimensions of individualism versus collectivism, and on uncertainty avoidance.

Individualism/Collectivism – the US is an example of an individualist culture, where the focus tends towards the individual first, and the immediate family second. In collectivist cultures (e.g. the Middle and Far East), from birth to death, people are integrated into strong, cohesive groups, represented by the extended family and socio-cultural group. These on one side supply support and connection. However the results of not fitting in and striking a decidedly individualist course can result in severe sanctions and exclusion from the group – even, in extremis, death. The argument that "it's my life and I'll use it to do what I like, and in my own way" – a clear boundary between the individual and society – is distinctly western in its cultural orientation. It contrasts with the connectedness of many traditional societies. (*Use examples from your own culture and/or those you know to develop and illustrate this point*)

This is also reflected in work ethics: in the US one can leave a job as soon as another one with better prospects and benefits comes up. In Japan, there is group and company loyalty; you stay with the company you are part of. In the US, a mistake costing the company millions of dollars means instant dismissal for the employee concerned. In Japan, the company may well take the error in its stride, covering up for the employee, especially if he has established himself as trustworthy and "one of the company".

Uncertainty avoidance – implies the span of a society's comfort zones, and willingness to stray out its comfort zones to reap the potential rewards. North America's culture (and the IB's culture) is that constructive risk-taking is a necessity for developing academic and social maturity, and that learning from mistakes is a positive experience. Going bankrupt, as long as the business has been run in good faith, is par for the course for a first-time business-person. In Europe it can have serious connotations, such as great difficulties in obtaining credit for future ventures. Similarly, companies face the cultural issue when deciding where to introduce new products. For example, when Visa introduced credit cards in the UK in the 1960s, the more risk-taking London area took to them in a big way. The Welsh seemed to hate the stuff – "cash only, here".

Uncertainty-avoidance cultures attempt to keep the society as safe and secure as possible, with the outlook that "there is only one Truth, and we are the people that have it".

Using one or more examples, explain 'emic' and 'etic' concepts.

The founding fathers of psychology took a very western view to behaviors, They attempted to find universal behaviors, taking for granted that they would apply to human beings worldwide. This is the **etic approach.** In contrast, the **emic approach** looks at behavior that is culturally specific – and as a result, many studies have had to be adapted to take in the culture factor.

For example, different schools have different cultures, expectations, written rules, and unwritten norms of behavior. Comparing schools using uniform criteria in academic achievement, sporting and music facilities, standards of classroom discipline, and how happy the students are is etic. It assumes that all schools are in the same cultural framework. However, there are subtle cultural differences between schools. School A might score higher on the happiness scale, according to etic criteria. But the culture of School B is that good schooling is not meant to be enjoyable. An emic approach would include that point in determining the school's overall efficacy.

Moreover, those criteria may not even be appropriate for school B, as they simply do not fit the school's orientation. An emic approach would identify the school on its own terms and set the criteria as appropriate to the school. Service to the community, or stringent religious conformity might be closer to the school's own perception of success.

Etic studies to the study of depression – for example, the WHO (World Health Organization) 1983 investigation of the diagnosis and classification of depression in Switzerland, Canada, Japan, and Iran. The study identified the symptoms reported by most of the over-500 patients studied in those four countries. These included sadness, joylessness, anxiety, and a sense of insufficiency.

The etic approach of that study (and its consequent limitations) was underlined when further investigation of the sample showed that nearly half of the patients displayed symptoms of somatic complaints and obsessions that were not within the scope of the symptoms measured by the study. Thus the meaning of 'depression' has different connotations to different cultures. Depressive symptoms are not experienced the same way in all cultures. Indeed, the Chinese often tend to report depression in terms of somatic symptoms, such as body pains and upsets (Draguns & Tanaka-Matsumi, 2003).

Emic studies to the study of depression – for example, Manson et al. (1985), on depressive illness amongst the Hopi tribe of American Indians. Most Hopi participants could not identify a Hopi word which translated into depression. But they were all familiar with the Hopi mind-disturbance categories, including worry sickness, unhappiness, heartbroken, drunken-like craziness, and disappointment. Some of those characteristics identified by the Hopi followed the western perception. Others, for example 'heartbroken', on investigation were very different to the western understanding. Heartbroken to the Hopi meant weight-loss, fatigue, loss of sexual appetite, trouble thinking clearly, and feelings of not being likeable.

Thus although depression appears to be a universal phenomenon, its development and expression are culturally determined. Indeed, **the work of Marsella et al. (2002)** suggests that depression is expressed differently according to whether the culture is individualist or collective. In individualist societies, it comes out in feelings of loneliness and isolation. In collective societies, it comes out in somatic symptoms such as headaches and dizziness.

POSSIBLE EXAMINATION QUESTIONS

SHORT ANSWER QUESTIONS

Describe one study relevant to social identity theory.

Explain any two compliance techniques..

LONG ANSWER QUESTIONS

Evaluate research on conformity to group norms.

Examine the role of two cultural dimensions on behavior.

CHAPTER FOUR – ABNORMAL PSYCHOLOGY

Paper 2 – option topic

Remember that you are applying the biological, cognitive, and socio-cultural perspectives to specific issues within the field of abnormal psychology.

Abnormal psychology in this program looks at three areas: anxiety disorders, affective disorders, and eating disorders. Our focus will be on anxiety disorders and eating disorders.

The goal of abnormal psychology is to identify the causes of abnormal behavior, and consider how to treat them most effectively - whether by clinical and/or therapeutic means.

Learning outcomes of this unit: general framework (applicable to all topics in the option)

To what extent do biological, cognitive and socio-cultural factors influence abnormal behavior?

For biological influences, look at the following:

- Medical criteria used in defining and diagnosing abnormality.
- The work of Fernald & Gunnar (2008) on the cortisol hypothesis in depression.
- The role of genetics in causing psychological disorders: the work of Kendler et al. (1991)
- The work of Leuchter et al. (2002) in assessing both the use of medication and the use of placebos in helping recovery from the depression.

For cognitive influences, look at the following:

- The ease of cognitive-based error in diagnosis: the research of Rosenhan (1973) "On being sane in insane places".
- Beck's cognitive theory of depression (1976)
- The body-image distortion hypothesis as causes of bulimia nervosa.
- The study of Elkin et al. (1989) on the success of different means of treating major depression, including the cognitive CBT.

For socio-cultural influences, look at the following:

- Socio-cultural criteria used in defining and diagnosing abnormality.
- The issue of cultural variation in the diagnostic process.
- The work of Brown & Harris (1978) in investigating the social causes of depression.
- The work of Levine et al. (1994) in investigating the role of social pressure creating at risk conditions for bulimia nervosa.
- The work of Kyuken et al. (2008) investigating the effectiveness of MBCT as an alternative to medication in treatment of depression.

Evaluate psychological research (that is, theories and/or studies) relevant to abnormal behavior.

For concepts and diagnosis, look at the following:

- The work of Beck et al. (1962), and Cooper et al. (1972) in investigating reliability in the diagnosis of depression and schizophrenia.
- The ease of error in diagnosis: the research of Rosenhan (1973) "On being sane in insane places".

For psychological disorders, look at the following:

- The work of Fernald & Gunnar (2008) on the cortisol hypothesis in depression.
- The role of genetics in causing psychological disorders: the work of Kendler et al. (1991) on bulimia nervosa.
- Beck's cognitive theory of depression (1976).
- The body-image distortion hypothesis as causes of bulimia nervosa.
- The work of Brown & Harris (1978) in investigating the social causes of depression.
- The work of Levine et al. (1994) in investigating the role of social pressure creating at risk conditions for bulimia nervosa.

For implementing treatment, look at the following:

- The work of Leuchter et al. (2002) in assessing both the use of medication and the use of placebos in helping recovery from the depression.
- The study of Elkin et al. (1989) on the success of different means of treating major depression.
- The work of Kyuken et al. (2008) investigating the effectiveness of MBCT as an alternative to medication.

SECTION ONE – CONCEPTS AND DIAGNOSIS

Examine the concepts of normality and abnormality.

Normality is defined by Jahoda (1958) in terms of the components of ideal mental health, which include:

(a) Self-esteem: a positive attitude to yourself. Even if you know you're far from perfect. You have a realistic and positive perception of who you are.
(b) Personal growth: you see yourself on the way to positive goals. You are becoming a greater person in your own way, not in somebody else's way. Your life is mainly growth, development, and self-actualization.
(c) Environmental mastery: you feel that you can cope and positively interact with the situations and people around you. Your independence gives you both the choices and the resources to cope with routine situations and stressful situations.
(d) Interaction with others: you can form and develop deepening relationships, including romantic ones.
(e) Integration: you can fit into your surroundings without sacrificing your identity.

Substantial deviations from any these norms would suggest abnormality.

In fact, this list seems to describe the characteristics of particular well-adapted individuals who would be a minority in society. These ideas may be challenged by:

(i) The list is a summary of the ideals, rather than the realities of Western society.

(ii) The list is culturally Western. The norm of people in many societies is to turn to superiors and cultural tradition for advice, rather than to their own assessment of the situations and to their own coping strategies.
(iii) Many people's perception of who they are is not positive and realistic, but over-positive and unrealistic. That would hardly be abnormal, even though it is a faulty self-perception.

Abnormally has been defined in terms of 'illness in the psyche'. This is based on medical diagnosis – psychiatry is a branch of medicine. Thus a mental disorder may be classified as an illness, as would be a physical disorder.

Most psychological disorders cannot be traced to physiological (biological) disorders, despite advances in brain-scanning technology. Indeed, the psychiatric diagnosis of mental illness relies on professionally-produced diagnostic manuals (for classification purposes), clinical interviews, and the patients' self-reporting. Its issues include:

(i) The possibility of a diagnosis causing the patient to suffer the stigma of mental illness.
(ii) The patient diagnosed as mentally ill being no longer held fully responsible for often violent or anti-social behavior.
(iii) The lack of medical evidence in diagnosis of most conditions, due to the difficulties in understanding the workings of the brain.
(iv) Serious errors can occur in diagnosis – see the study of Rosenhan (1973) below 'on being sane in insane places.'

Abnormality has been defined by Rosenhan and Seligman (1984) as including seven criteria to determine whether a person or a behavior pattern is normal or not:

(a) Is any suffering involved?
(b) Is the person's behavior the source of his or her own troubles?
(c) Does the person manage to communicate his feelings in a rational and reasonable way?
(d) Is an unpredictable pattern shown in dealing with situations?
(e) Is a particular situation experienced quite differently from the ways others go through it?
(f) Is the behavior causing awkwardness and embarrassment to others?
(g) Is the person's way of doing things in violation of his/her accepted cultural standards?

This list shows a careful balance between the mental well-being of the individual and the realities of society at large. However, it needs to take into account that social (and political) realities change:

(i) The work of Read et al (2004) exemplifies behavior that would not be considered abnormal today, but was once. Examples include a sexual interest in a person of the same gender, and a woman deliberately choosing to be single rather than marry.
(ii) The behavior of the person may be categorized as abnormal when it is seen to threaten powerfully-backed regimes and interests. For example, the Soviets' categorizing of dissidents as mentally abnormal and forcing them to undergo clinical treatment.
(iii) Many behaviors at odds with the dominant culture are normal conduct for the minority-culture that the individual identifies with. This is exemplified in the manual of the American Psychiatric Association (DSM-IV-TR – see below), which classifies various disorders as 'culture-bound syndromes'.

Discuss the validity and reliability of diagnosis.

Diagnosis is the identification of disease on the basis of symptoms, clinical tests, observations, interviewing those connected with the patient, and information from the patient.

There are several systems of classification of identifiable mental disorder. Two of them are:

- The American Psychiatric Association's *Diagnostic and Statistical Manual of Mental Disorders* (DSM-IV-TR) – fifth edition due for release in 2013. The constant revision is designed to make diagnosis more reliable, by including the most recent developments in medical and psychological knowledge. Since 1987, this source has shown increasing awareness of viewing people's problems more holistically, within an integrated bio-psycho-medical framework.
- *The International Classification of Diseases* (ICD-10) – now in its tenth edition. A product of WHO (World Health Organization), its section on mental disease is becoming increasingly similar to the DSM.

What does and does not constitute a disorder has varied over time. Homosexuality was no longer classified as a disorder after 1980, and since then there have been several changes in what and what does not constitute an eating disorder.

Also, the amount of focus on a particular disorder can change over time. For example, following a public awareness campaign sponsored by GlaxoSmithKline in promoting Paxil as a drug that could treat shyness, social anxiety became the third most diagnosed mental illness.

The psychological profession uses the ABCS framework of describing the symptoms of a disorder, which forms the basis of a diagnosis:

(a) Affective symptoms – emotional elements such as euphoria, sadness, fear.
(b) Behavioral symptoms – observations such as excessive laughter, weeping, looking away in conversation.
(c) Cognitive symptoms – such as personalization (attempting to give a false impression of who you really are).
(d) Somatic symptoms – such as 'butterflies in the stomach', stomach cramps, sudden jerky movements.

Issues affecting the reliability of diagnosis – (different psychiatrists should make the same correct diagnosis if they use the same diagnostic procedures).

(i) The standardization of manuals (above) which define and specify symptoms to look for helps reliability. It still does place the responsibility on the individual psychiatrist to **decide whether the degree of severity of the patient's symptoms actually meets the criteria for the diagnosis**. Inaccurate diagnosis could negatively label the patient, affect his/her job, require medical treatment and even hospitalization, rather than the symptoms simply being an individual's coping strategy with life's difficulties. This argument might well be less important with the advance of brain scanning technology, especially in the diagnosis of conditions such as Alzheimer's disease, and ADD / ADHD (attention-deficit disorder / attention-deficit-hyperactivity disorder).

(ii) Differences in the style, theoretical orientation, and personality of the clinical interviewer. For example, the work of Cooper et al. (1972) sought to investigate reliability in the diagnosis of depression and schizophrenia. It involved American and British psychiatrists observing movies of clinical interviews of patients, whom they had to diagnose. Twice as many of those viewed were diagnosed as schizophrenic by the American psychiatrists as by the British psychiatrists.

(iii) Value judgments are involved in psychiatric diagnosis that can depend on the values and the culture of both the interviewer and the patient, as opposed to the more objective criteria of medical diagnosis.

(iv) Difficulty in distinguishing between normal and abnormal behavior in reality. The work of Rosenhan (1973) "On being sane in insane places" sought to test the reliability and validity of diagnosis of schizophrenia in an ecologically valid setting. Could psychiatrists distinguish between 'normal' and 'abnormal' behavior?

Each of the eight participants (including Rosenhan himself) was to attempt to gain admission to a specific psychiatric hospital (a total of 12, within the USA). This was done by claiming to have heard 'voices', but otherwise giving a normal background. The ruse worked. All instances were diagnosed as schizophrenia, except one which was classified as manic depression.

Once admitted, their aim was to be discharged as soon as possible – which was dependent on their convincing the staff that they were sufficiently mentally healthy. They thus acted perfectly normally when hospitalized, except for taking notes. That was vital. For all the participants were observing the hospital staff without their knowledge (covert observer participation).

In fact, the note-taking was interpreted as evidence of insanity by the staff members, who did not seem to pay much attention to the content of the notes. On average, it took 19 days for them to be released, most commonly with a diagnosis of 'schizophrenia in remission'. (The findings caused considerable embarrassment to the psychiatric profession.)

The follow-up study took place when the staff at one psychiatric hospital was told that some fake patients would present themselves, and they should be on the lookout for them. Out of 193 patients, 43 were rejected by at least one member of staff. In fact all the patients were genuine.

Strengths of Rosenhan

(a) Ecologically valid – and no issues in determining cause (the faked hearing of 'voices') and the effect (the admission to the psychiatric ward as a patient).
(b) Highlighted the need to improve existing diagnostic tools, including the manuals.

Criticisms of Rosenhan

(a) Needs to address the ethical issues of covert participant observation. May well be justifiable in this case as the findings were of paramount public importance and could not have been obtained in any other way.
(b) The word that imposters would be present in the follow-up study raises the ethical issue of genuine patients not receiving necessary treatment.

Discuss cultural and ethical considerations in diagnosis *(for example, cultural variation, stigmatization)*

Cultural considerations in diagnosis – the issue of cultural variation

The differences in cultures between the psychiatrist and the patient may create severe difficulties in effective psychiatric diagnosis:

(a) There is a fear of giving a diagnosis of (for example) depression, as it can create disproportionate harm to the patient in his/her own society (stigmatization, see below). It can make the patient extremely wary of reporting affective, behavioral, and cognitive symptoms.

(b) There is the possibility that the distress that the person experiences is a product of the belief system. Mental suffering is the divine-imposed consequence of a past misdeed, rather than a fundamental underlying disorder. This may influence the patient to play down the symptoms and thus be at risk of not receiving an appropriate diagnosis and treatment.

(c) There is the possibility of the psychiatrist not being able to identify signs of (for example) depression that are expressed in a non-recognizable way in a different ethnic group. Some cultures tend to play down emotionally-expressed disorders, and only address them when they are expressed somatically. For example, the study of Zhang et al. (1998) reported that only 16 out of over 19,000 people from twelve different regions in China reported suffering from a mood disorder at least once in their life. This might indicate that depression hardly exists amongst the Chinese. However, many did report *somatic* symptoms that indicated depression, such as 'a weakness of the nerves' 'fatigue' and often 'lower-back pains'. That fits in with the Chinese emphasis on disease arising out of disharmony in the body between the 'energy flow' and the different organs in the body. Indeed, the work of Kleinman (1984) argued that the somatization of symptoms makes it difficult to 'join the dots' and identify a depressive situation even where one exists. There is also the consequent danger of too readily accepting physical pain by itself as a symptom of depression with Chinese patients.

These cultural issues may be addressed by the psychiatrist working together with a bilingual person trained in mental health. He or she can relate and present the various symptoms reported by the patient to the framework of the psychiatrist's understanding.

Ethical considerations in diagnosis – the issue of stigmatization

The reality of psychiatric diagnosis is that it gives the patient a new identity, which can be a label for life, such as 'schizophrenic' or 'depressive', rather than (as DSM-IV recommends) 'a person with schizophrenia' or 'a person with depression'. This is a stigma that can continue after the symptoms are over: 'schizophrenia in remission' and 'depression in remission'. It is very likely to affect marriage prospects, job prospects, and indeed his or her sense of personal identity. The work of Doherty (1975) points out that those who reject their mental illness label tend to improve more quickly than those who accept it.

The ethical difficulties are all the more serious where members of certain groups are at higher risk of receiving a stigmatizing diagnosis than others, including:

(a) In the UK, a patient is nine times as likely to be diagnosed as being schizophrenic if coming from an Afro-Caribbean background rather than from a white British one. Morgan et al. (2006) account for this with racially-biased diagnostic error rather than genetics.

(b) Women are more likely to be diagnosed with depression. The work of Rosser (1992) argues that be partially due to the large number of male psychiatrists in the profession who might 'over-diagnose' and stigmatize a woman as being depressed. In reality she could be bored and frustrated with her role as a mother and homemaker, and misses her honored role in the workplace.

Ethically, there remains the very grave issue of the risk of over-diagnosis and the unjust consequences flowing from stigmatization (including 'in remission' conditions) needing to be balanced with the potential denial of treatment to those who need it, which can prevent a suicide or grievous bodily harm to a third party.

SECTION TWO – PSYCHOLOGICAL DISORDERS

Describe symptoms and prevalence of one disorder from the following groups: affective disorders, eating disorders.

Affective disorders are those which relate to mood – one example being major depression (lasting more than two weeks, in an extreme case about two years, and on average recurring four times).

Major depression affects about 15% of the population (Charney & Weismann 1988). In the UK, some 25% of admissions to psychiatric hospitals are because of diagnosed depression. Its main symptoms are:

  (a) Affective symptoms – distress, lack of signs of interest or pleasure.
  (b) Behavioral symptoms – not wishing to be together with other people, difficulty in sleeping at night, difficulty in getting through a normal day's work, observable agitated or unusually slow movements, self-destructive and even suicidal behavior.
  (c) Cognitive symptoms – problems in staying focused on what is going on, inappropriate feelings of guilt, and negative attitudes to oneself and one's surroundings.
  (d) Somatic symptoms – fatigue, loss of appetite, and significant weight loss or significant weight gain.

The prevalence (the number of people affected by a disorder at least once a lifetime) of major depression is a subject of many studies, including:

- In the USA, 13% for men, and 20% for women (Kessler et al. 2005).
- In Japan, prevalence is only 3% - only about one sixth of the USA (Andrade & Caraveo, 2003)
- In the city of Chennai, Southern India, the overall rate was 16%. It was more than three times as high with those having lower incomes than with those having high incomes. Over a quarter of those divorced had suffered or were suffering from major depression – higher than those widowed (one fifth), and those currently married (just over one seventh). (Poongothai et al., 2009, using a sample of 25,000 people and using a self-reporting questionnaire.)
- Depression is as prevalent with Jewish men as with Jewish women (Levav, 1997).

Eating disorders: for example, bulimia nervosa is where a person feels loss of control and self-disgust over eating too much high calorie food. He or (far more commonly) she prevents putting on weight by use of laxative tablets, induced vomiting, or excessive exercise. Its main symptoms are:

  (a) Affective symptoms – disliking the shape of one's body, fear of putting on weight.
  (b) Behavioral symptoms – cycles of feasting and desperate attempts to get rid of excess weight.
  (c) Cognitive symptoms – negatively distorted body image, low self-esteem accompanied by a depressed mood.
  (d) Somatic symptoms – nutritional deficiencies leading to hormonal imbalances, muscle cramping, tiredness, and disruptions in the menstrual cycle.

More women than men have bulimia. The disorder is most common in adolescent girls and young women.

The prevalence of bulimia is a subject of many studies, including:

- In the USA, 1%-2% for young women (Fairburn and Beglin, 1990), and much rarer - about 0.2% - for young men (Drewnowski et al. 1988). Drewnowski's study also found that bulimia was at its highest on university campuses (2.2% of the female undergraduates).
- In developing countries it is less frequent, but it still occurs. For example a questionnaire-based study of 351 secondary school girls in Egypt indicated that just over 1% filled the criteria for bulimia nervosa (Nasser, 1994).
- Overall, its prevalence seems to be on the increase (Keel & Klump, 2003 – based on surveying available research studies of bulimia). However, this should be balanced with the manuals' guidelines for diagnosis having become more definitive in the last few decades. Together with the practice of self-reporting, there are fewer barriers to be diagnosed as bulimic.

Analyze etiologies (in terms of biological, cognitive and/or socio-cultural factors) of one disorder from the following groups: affective disorders (e.g. major depression), and eating disorders (e.g. bulimia nervosa).

Etiology involves the explaining of the cause of the abnormal behavior. Etiology connects to psychiatry in that the treatment given should take into account the causes of the disorder. These may be biologically, cognitively, and/or socio-culturally rooted.

Etiologies of an affective disorder – major depression

Biological issues – the cortisol hypothesis: too much, or too little cortisol is associated with depression. Cortisol is a hormone which is naturally released to cope with a stress situation. Those suffering from chronic stress (stress prolonged over a long period) have high cortisol levels, which are associated with depression. High cortisol levels lower the density of serotonin receptors and the functioning of receptors for noradrenaline – associated with major depression.

Low levels of serotonin are also associated with low levels of enjoyment, including major depression When in constant demand during a long period of chronic stress, cortisol begins to run out. The work of Fernald & Gunnar (2008) surveyed over 600 Mexican mothers and their children, in different socio-economic groups. It found that those living in the worst poverty were producing the least stress-coping cortisol. Their stress-coping biological mechanism tended to be worn out, leaving the children open to depression and also more open to poor-immunization-based diseases, such as multiple-sclerosis.

In evaluation, the cortisol hypothesis (excessive cortisol and insufficient cortisol) has been supported by studies such as Fernald & Gunnar above (low cortisol), and also the high incidence of depression amongst those with very high cortisol levels (Cushing's syndrome). Indeed, the use of medication to lower cortisol levels in Cushing's syndrome appears to have caused the depression to disappear – though cause and effect has not been fully established.

Biological issues – genetic predisposition: depression rates are most likely to be similar amongst those sharing the highest degree of common genetic material. Thus the depression rate concordance in MZ (monozygotic) twins is likely to be higher than in DZ (dizygotic) twins. The work of Sullivan (2000) combined previous research studies, involving a total of

21,000 twins. This indicated that a MZ twin was more than twice as likely to develop depression if the other twin had it, than a DZ twin. This reflected the greater amount of common genetic material shared by the MZ twins. However, the study showed that different environmental factors experienced by each twin were also important.

Cognitive issues – depressogenic schemas (negative cognitive schemas): is negative thinking a cause of depression or a symptom of depression?

Beck's cognitive theory of depression (1976) is based on the negative schemas which developed out of negative experiences in childhood and early adolescence – with parents and other people of importance. Suffering persistent rejection in childhood or later on can lead to feelings of worthlessness as an adult. Being rejected plays the sound track of "everyone hates me, I'll never be accepted". It will cause negative feelings about oneself, which in turn will play the sound track of: "I am useless. I am worthless. I am good-for-nothing". Both sound tracks interact to create a negative schema in processing one's environment, creating the combined message: "everyone hates me because I am worthless".

In other words, Beck observed that depressive patients show evidence of a distorted cognitive set of schemas about the self, about the future, and about what is going on all around.

In evaluation: it creates a framework to show how those suffering depression think more negatively about themselves and the world even when they are not actually depressed. For the depressogenic schema remains. This would strengthen Beck's assertion that it is the negative schema that is a cause of depression, rather than a product of a depression. On the other hand, it does not rule out the depressogenic schema being a product of depression as well as a cause of depression.

Socio-cultural issues – one's social environment and circumstances, such poverty, an unsatisfactory relationship with spouse, or lack of social support can cause depression.

The work of Brown & Harris (1978) in south-east London investigated the social causes of depression. The semi-structured-interview-based study was confined to two groups of women. One group contained women who had sought/received help for depression, and the second group was a general sample of 458 women between ages 18 and 65. The findings of the study included:
(i) Over four-fifths of the first group had suffered a major life-cycle-event (such as a death of a close relative) or a prolonged severe difficulty (e.g. coping with the children at home), compared with only a third of those who were not in a depressed group.
(ii) There were poverty-linked tendencies to depression in the second group. Those in the poorer, working class showed 23% to have been depressed at least once in the last twelve months. That contrasted with just 3% in the more affluent middle class.
(iii) Substantially higher rates of depression were found in women who were separated, divorced, or widowed, than those who were married.

In evaluation – this shows that social factors seem to cause depression, irrespective of biologically-rooted and cognitively-rooted personality factors. The semi-structured interview helped to pin-point the stressors most linked to the cause of depression. Indeed, the etiology of a depression today often includes social factors.

However, this study was confined to women – creating difficulties in generalizing it to men. There were also difficulties of establishing cause and effect – for example, did poverty create the depression, or did the depression create the poverty?

Etiologies in an eating disorder – bulimia nervosa

Biological issues – genetic predisposition: the work of Kendler et al. (1991) studied the incidence of bulimia in over 2,000 female twins. It found a higher rate of concordance of bulimia nervosa (23%) in MZ twins than in DZ twins (9%). This indicated that a MZ twin was more than twice as likely to develop bulimia if the other twin had it, than a DZ twin. That reflected the greater amount of common genetic material shared by the MZ twins.

In evaluation, the study does indicate a heredity factor, by it being more than twice as pronounced in the DZ twins that are sharing more genetic material. The sample (over 2,000) was a large one. The limitations include the study's being confined to women not being readily generalized to (the relatively rare) male bulimia, and the role of social factors common to both twins that underlie bulimia development.

Cognitive issues – the body-image distortion hypothesis, and the weight-related schema model

The body-image distortion hypothesis) is that many bulimic people suffer from the cognitive delusion that they are fat. **This is supported by the work of Fallon & Rozin (1985)** in the United States, which tested the degree of body-image distortion in 474 male and female college undergraduates. Both males and females were given pictures of nine body shapes, from very thin to very heavy. The participants were required to select the body shape (i) most similar to their own, (ii) most similar to their ideal body shape, and (iii) what body shape in the opposite sex they found most attractive. Men tended to choose the same body shape all three times. Women thought themselves heavier than the most attractive body shape, and they chose a much thinner idealized body shape. That indicates much cognitive stress caused by the gap between the way women perceive their figure, and the actual figure they would like to be.

Socio-cultural issues – highlights that body shape is a major criterion in the way people evaluate themselves and in the way people evaluate others. This puts social pressure on those who do not achieve their perceived body ideal, putting them at risk for eating disorders including bulimia nervosa.

Movie stars and fashion models promote trends for the ideal body shape. So do some types of toy dolls on the market. The work of Sanders and Bazalgette (1993) looked at the bust-waist-hips ratios of the popular Barbie, Sindy, and Little Mermaid dolls. They found their proportions to be caricatures of the idealized female body shape at that time in the media.

The work of Levine et al. (1994) researched the relationship between social attitudes experienced by nearly 400 10-14 year old girls in the USA and their attitudes and behavior towards food. Their questionnaire responses highlighted that:

(i) They received powerful messages to be slim – from fashion magazines, friends, and family.
(ii) Many received strong home encouragement to develop a slim figure, and suffered criticism and teasing.
(iii) Their sources encouraged dieting and exercise to develop and maintain an ideal slim figure.

This suggests that social pressure is a means of putting people at risk for development of bulimia nervosa. To that end, the State of Israel passed a law in March 2012 that neither male nor female with the over-slim BMI (body-mass index, see chapter 6) below 18.5 may be employed in Israel as a model.

Discuss cultural and gender variations in prevalence of disorders.

For major depression...

Reminder! The prevalence (the number of people affected by a disorder at least once a lifetime) of major depression is a subject of many studies, including:

- In the USA, 13% for men, and 20% for women (Kessler et al. 2005).
- In Japan, prevalence is only 3% - only about one sixth of the USA (Andrade & Caraveo, 2003)
- In the city of Chennai, Southern India, the overall rate was 16%. It was more than three times as high with those having lower incomes than with those having high incomes. Over a quarter of those divorced had suffered or were suffering from major depression – higher than those widowed (one fifth), and those currently married (just over one seventh). (Poongothai et al., 2009, using a sample of 25,000 people and using a self-reporting questionnaire.)
- Depression is as prevalent with Jewish men as with Jewish women (Levav, 1997). However, this is exceptional, and not shown to be true amongst other populations.

Culturally, in addition...

The work of Weisman (1996) involved a cross-cultural study of the prevalence of depression in ten locations worldwide. Heading the list was recently war-torn Beirut, Lebanon (19%), with peaceful Paris, France not far behind at 16%. The Far Eastern island of Taiwan showed the lowest rate at 1.5% - just over half of that of neighbor South Korea at 2.9%.

This should be viewed in the context of the rising global rates of major depression. Major depression seems to be the world's most prevalent psychiatric disorder (Marsella, 2002). Rising rates are attributed to many causes include difficulties in adjusting to the rapid changes in modern living, rapid urbanization, poverty and cultural collapse. It should also bear in mind that the statistical variations in depression may well be under-reporting the real situation, as:

(a) The stigma of reporting and diagnosis varies worldwide – where it is high in e.g. China, people tend to report depression symptoms somatically – emphasizing physical pain (Satortius et al, 1983).
(b) The geographical process of urbanization (rural-urban migration) means that a greater percentage of the world's population lives in cities and with it, the unfamiliar strains of city life. These include living in overcrowded accommodation, underemployment (earning insufficient for basic living standards), and insufficient adaptation skills to cope with the rapid change of modern living. Access to psychiatric systems could be beyond the reach of those lacking urban navigation skills and basic literacy (Marsella, 1995).

Gender-wise, in addition...

Women being twice as likely as men to develop major depression is not related to different gender-related procedures in diagnosis (Piccinelli & Wilkinson, 2000). The gender differences are almost completely the same cross-culturally. Explanations for women being more susceptible to major depression include:

(a) Different biological mechanisms in coping with stress, reflected in the way they think about themselves, and the styles they use to handle difficulties (Nolen-Hoeksema,

2001). Chronic stress can lead to being vulnerable to depression – expressed in Beck's schema of depression.

(b) Socio-culturally: women's relatively low social status in many societies, which comes with poorer access to resources, the brunt of the hard work of child-rearing, the chronic strains and frustrations of being a housewife and mother, sexual abuse, and poverty (Nolen-Hoeksema, 2001).

For bulimia nervosa...

Reminder! The prevalence of bulimia nervosa is a subject of many studies, including:

- In the USA, 1%-2% for young women (Fairburn and Beglin, 1990), and much rarer - about 0.2%) - for young men (Drewnowski et al. 1988). Drewnowski's study also found that bulimia was at its highest on university campuses (2.2% of the female undergraduates).
- In developing countries it is less frequent, but it still occurs. For example a questionnaire-based study of 351 secondary school girls in Egypt indicated that just over 1% filled the criteria for bulimia nervosa (Nasser, 1994).
- Overall, its prevalence seems to be on the increase (Keel & Klump, 2003 – based on surveying available research studies of bulimia). However, this should be balanced with the manuals' guidelines for diagnosis having become more definitive in the last few decades. Together with the practice of self-reporting, there are fewer barriers to be diagnosed as bulimic.

Culturally, explanations for the prevalence of bulimia include the globalization of culture. This involves imposing western ideals on the ideal body shape - being socially reinforced worldwide through slim female figures on globalized television, movies, and women's magazines. That puts social pressure on women worldwide to conform to the model of the 'affluent and successful Western society'. **This is emphasized by the work of Becker et al (2002)** on the prevalence of bulimia in adolescent girls in a remote area of the Fiji Islands before the then introduction of TV (1995), and three years after the introduction of TV (1998). The study used a questionnaire and follow-up semi-structured interviews on girls' eating patterns from two secondary schools. The results indicated that there had been a change in the ideal body profile from fairly round and robust before television introduction, to the slim western model afterwards. There was no dieting before the introduction of TV. Three years later, more than 10% of the girls reported dieting and self-induced vomiting as a means of working towards the western-idealized body shape.

Male incidences of bulimia nervosa were less frequent (below 10% of the female rate), with explanations including less social pressure for men to achieve an ideal physical profile. However, the study of Silberstein et al, 1989 identified two categories of men with some chance of developing this disorder: those involved in weight-bound activities (such as jockeys), and those in the homosexual communities which place a higher emphasis on good looks.

SECTION THREE – IMPLEMENTING TREATMENT

Examine biomedical, individual, and group approaches to treatment.
and
Evaluate the use of biomedical, individual and group approaches to the treatment of one disorder (for example, major depression).

Biomedical treatment involves the use of appropriate drugs to restore the body to health where the etiology of the depression indicates biological roots. Low levels of the neurotransmitter serotonin (see earlier in this chapter) are characteristic of depression. Therefore biomedical treatment should aim to restore serotonin activity to normal levels. This approach has been used to treat bulimia nervosa, as many sufferers have developed major depression at the same time.

The biological approach almost always involves the use of drugs – typically anti-depressants. Commonly used to restore serotonin levels are SSRIs (serotonin re-uptake inhibitors). These make each unit of neurotransmitter serotonin more effective. Instead of the serotonin being immediately reabsorbed, it stays longer in the synaptic gaps, and is therefore more effective as a unit of pleasure. The aim is to improve serotonin-based energy, lifting the depression.

However, they directly address the symptoms of major depression (low serotonin levels) rather than the causes of major depression.

SSRI users also face the risk of the side-effects of nausea, headaches, insomnia, and sexual problems.

The work of Leuchter et al. (2002) assessed both the use of SSRIs and the use of placebos (substances the patient believed to be anti-depressant, but were not designed to have any effect at all) in helping recovery from the depression. This study divided 51 depression patients into two groups. The first group was given SSRIs. The second was given placebos. Both groups were EEG brain-scanned. The scans showed substantial frontal-cortex activity with those taking placebos. Those on SSRIs did not show the same frontal-cortex activity, but both groups recovered from depression.

This study indicates that although the SSRIs address only the symptoms of the depression, the belief that they are genuine treatment may well set the brain off into depression-recovery mode. The same could be said of placebos, although the differences in frontal cortex activity indicate that the depression-recovery process is by a different route.

Strengths of Leuchter et al.

- The findings are scientifically supported from the brain-scanning results.
- The findings were quantitatively supported by the sample size.
- The success of placebos in treating depression has been supported by later studies (including Kirsch et al. 2008).

Limitations of Leuchter et al.

- The information the scans send in the form of colors may exaggerate the different activities in the brain.
- The brain areas might light up on the machine for different reasons than those supposed by the investigator.
- It seems to conflict with findings of the study of Elkin (1989, see below), which showed a substantially lower recovery rate from those on placebos. It could be that those taking part in Elkin's study were in more severe major depressions, for whom placebos would be less effective.

Individual (cognitive) treatment can involve CBT (cognitive behavioral therapy). Its etiology is that negative thinking is a cause rather than just a symptom of depression (see above). Reminder: it works on the basis that suffering persistent rejection in childhood or later on can lead to feelings of worthlessness as an adult. Being rejected plays the sound track of "everyone hates me, I'll never be accepted". It will cause negative feelings about oneself, which in turn will play the sound track of: "I am useless. I am worthless. I am good-for-nothing". Both sound tracks interact to build a negative schema in processing one's environment, creating the combined message: "everyone hates me because I am worthless". In other words, Beck observed that depressive patients show evidence of a distorted cognitive set of schemas about the self, about the future, and about what is going on all around.

CBT therapy operates on a one-to-one basis. It seeks to enable the depressed person to (i) identify what the negative beliefs and thinking patterns are (ii) test out whether these beliefs are actually true – reality testing, and (iii) to accept that parts of the thinking patterns are flawed. It moves on to activities that produce positive feelings, seeking more positive problem-solving means. The whole process of CBT for a major-depressed patient can involve some 20 sessions.

The study of Elkin et al. (1989) was an outcome-focused study on the success of different means of treating major depression. 280 patients participated, and were allocated randomly into four groups: (i) biomedical treatment – anti-depressants plus normal clinical management (ii) supposed biomedical treatment – placebo plus normal clinical management (iii) CBT, and (iv) IPT (interpersonal psychotherapy, enables clients to identify their problems in relating to others as these are felt to be a root cause of depression). The treatment lasted for four months. Patients were assessed three times: before treatment, after six weeks of treatment, and after a year-and-a-half. The results were that over half of those on medication, and those having received cognitive therapy (CBT and IPT) recovered. Only 29% of the placebo group got better. This suggests that both medication and psychotherapy work to some degree, but neither by themselves are even nearly successful for all those being treated for major depression.

Strengths of Elkin et al.

- The divisions into four groups ensured that the study was well-controlled.
- The findings were quantitatively supported by the sample size.

Limitations of Elkin al.

- The low success rate of placebos in treating depression is not supported by later studies, such as Leuchter et al. (2002) (above). Possibly, Elkin's sample had more severely depressed patients for whom placebos would have been less effective.
- It addressed the outcome of treatment for major depression, rather than the cause of major depression.

CBT is also widely used for bulimia nervosa. The treatment typically involves (i) identifying the negative beliefs and thinking patterns about the mental distortions on body shape (ii) identifying the negative behaviors of binge-eating and vomiting (iii) moving on to activities that produce more positive feelings about one's physical appearance: replace binge-eating and vomiting with three planned meals and two planned snacks per day (iv) working with people who are close and supportive to the patient to offer encouragement (v) maintaining the program to prevent relapse into bulimia.

The work of Fairburn (1995) demonstrated the efficacy of CBT, in that nearly two-thirds of the eating disorder-patients had not relapsed in the following five years.

Group therapy (socio-cultural) is where a therapist and other past and present sufferers (from both depression and eating disorders) participate in a discussion together. Present sufferers can feel more optimistic about their own chances of recovery if they are involved with those who have 'been there before' and managed to improve their own situation. They no longer feel alone, or solely reliant on the therapist. Indeed, the group therapy can turn into a support group.

The work of McDermut et al. (2001) indicates that group therapy is at least as successful for patients as individual therapy. However, it may be criticized as the most extreme sufferers of depression, or eating disorders are more likely to be treated individually rather than in groups. Though cheaper per patient than individualized CBT, groups frequently fall apart through disliking other patients in the group (who sometimes show inappropriate behavior and lack of respect to others).

Successful group therapy often incorporates MBCT. This may be defined as responding to the stress situation in a mentally-proactive manner, rather than reacting to it automatically. With repeated practice, the individual develops the capacity to **step back calmly from thoughts and feelings during stressful situations toward proactive coping strategy**, rather than negative thinking patterns that may escalate various stress responses.

The repeated practice may take several forms. It can include bodily scan (meditation practice – usually performed lying down, with the eyes closed – then direct attention to different parts of the body in turn – and focusing and accepting whatever sensation comes from each part). It can also include yoga exercises, where participants become aware of the body's different sensations, including those of tension and relaxation. It may include sitting meditation – uptight but relaxed posture, and focus on the physical sensation of breathing – allowing the mind to wander. The participant allows the mind to wander when it happens, but returns at once to breathing once more.

The participants are encouraged to bring mindfulness to their everyday lives – used when carrying out a daily routine such as a shower, the person is required to focus on the present moment, noticing the sensations experienced whilst doing it as in meditation.

The work of Kyuken et al. (2008) was a 15-month experimental study investigating the effectiveness of MBCT in a study of 123 depression-suffering participants with at least three episodes of depression. All participants were initially on anti-depressants, but instead of continuing on those drugs, the test group reduced medication and substituted MBCT. After the 15-month period, the medication stopped. The test group showed a relapse rate of 60%. The control group showed the substantially lower relapse rate of 47%. And those in the test group that received MCBT reported a much higher quality of life and feelings of physical well-being.

Strengths of Kyuken et al.

- The experimental nature of the study made it possible to show cause and effect. The findings were quantitatively supported by the sample size.
- The overall effectiveness of group therapy is supported by previous studies, such as that of McDermut et al, who combined 48 studies on the effectiveness of group therapy to demonstrate empirical evidence that group therapy can be effective as a means of enabling recovery from major depression.

Limitations of Kyuken et al.

- The study did not categorize the patients according to the severity of their major depression. Anyone suffering from three or more episodes of depression could have qualified.
- It addressed the outcome of treatment for major depression, rather than the cause of major depression.

Discuss the use of eclectic approaches to treatment.

An eclectic approach is where a person suffering from major depression, bulimia nervosa, or any other abnormal psychological condition is given more than one type of treatment, for example medication and CBT. Those involved in treatment combine their skills in working towards the patient's progress and recovery.

The study of Elkin et al. (1989) shows that no single method of treatment has a recovery success rate substantially higher than 50%.

The work of Pampallona et al. (2004) investigated how far the combination of biomedical and psychotherapy (including CBT and IPT) would improve the patient's chances of recovery from depression. Using 16 studies involving a total of nearly 2,000 patients, it compared the progress of patients receiving medication only, with the progress of patients receiving both medication and psychotherapy. The results showed the recovery rate going up to 70% (American National Institute of Mental Health).

Eclectic approaches can be an improvement on medication alone for the following reasons:

(a) Patients frequently do not continue to take medication regularly, reasons being unpleasant side effects, temporarily feeling better, or simply forgetting.
(b) Regular psychotherapy sessions involve 'touching base'- an incentive to keep on with the medication.

Discuss the relationship between etiology and therapeutic approach in relation to one disorder.

Etiology involves the explaining of the cause of the abnormal behavior. **Etiology connects to therapy in that the treatment given should take into account the causes of the disorder.** These may be biologically, cognitively, and/or socio-culturally rooted.

Overall, the causes of both major depression and bulimia nervosa are difficult to locate, and indeed appear to be multi-dimensional. That means that any approach to treating those psychological conditions is currently based on empirical results rather than a clear understanding of the etiology of the condition.

Despite the effectiveness of SSRIs in assisting recovery from depression, the link between low serotonin levels in the brain and depression (the serotonin hypothesis) is not yet proven. The success rate of anti-depressants (e.g. Paxil, Prozac) is based on empirical outcome results, rather than clear demonstration that blocking the serotonin reuptake capacity does actually address the depression.

The study of Elkin et al. (1989) (see above) showed that both medication and psychotherapy worked to some degree, but the empirical results did not address the serotonin hypothesis that low serotonin levels cause depression. Nor did the similar success rates with psychotherapeutic methods demonstrate an exclusively cognitive or social cause of depression. It could be argued that their success worked hand-in-hand with a natural healing of the condition, just as people recover from pneumonia without antibiotics.

POSSIBLE EXAMINATION QUESTIONS

LONG ANSWER QUESTIONS ONLY ON PAPER TWO

Discuss the validity and reliability of diagnosis of abnormality.

Discuss cultural and gender variations in prevalence of disorders.

Evaluate the use of *any two of* biomedical, individual and group approaches to the treatment of *one* disorder.

CHAPTER FIVE – DEVELOPMENTAL PSYCHOLOGY

Paper 2 – option topic

Remember that you are applying the biological, cognitive, and socio-cultural perspectives to specific issues within the field of developmental psychology.

Development psychology in this program looks at three areas: cognitive development, social development, and identity development.

The goal of developmental psychology is to gain an understanding of how early experience may influence later on in life, and if there are any critical periods in development.

Learning outcomes of this unit: General framework (applicable to all topics in the option)

To what extent do biological, cognitive and socio-cultural factors influence human development?

For biological influences, look at the following below:

- The neurobiological approach to human development.
- The Rutter et al. (2001) investigation of the long-term effects of severe deprivation in childhood on cognitive development and attachment disorder.
- Hormone-based psychosexual differentiation theory.

For cognitive influences, look at the following below:

- Piaget's theory of cognitive development.
- Bowlby's theory (1973) on the development of attachment.
- The study of Hazan and Shaver (1987) on adult styles of attachment relating to previous attachments made in infancy.
- Gender-schema theory.
- Erikson's theory of adolescent identity crisis.
- The investigation of Rutter et al (1976) on the reality of adolescent identity crisis.

For socio-cultural influences, look at the following below:

- Vygotsky's socio-cultural approach to cognitive development.
- The Michigan Department of Education (MDE) study (2002) on the effect of positive parenting on child cognitive development in evidence at school.
- The work of Schoon and Bartley (2008) in means of building resilience to deprivation and adversity.
- The work of Mead (1935) on different gender-roles in different tribes.
- The work of Ferron (1997) in comparing the way French adolescents and American adolescents related to their physical developments.

Evaluate psychological research (that is, theories and/or studies) relevant to developmental psychology.

For cognitive development, look at the following:

- The effect of deprivation on neuroplasticity (1997).

- Piaget's theory of cognitive development.
- Vysgotky's socio-cultural approach to cognitive development.
- The work of Bhoomika (2008) on the effects of malnourishment on the cognitive performance of elementary school children.
- The Michigan Department of Education (MDE) study (2002) on the effect of positive parenting on child cognitive development in evidence at school.
- The Rutter et al. (2001) investigation of the long-term effects of severe deprivation in childhood on cognitive development.

For social development, look at the following:

- Bowlby's theory (1973) on the development of attachment.
- The 'strange situation' study of Ainsworth et al. (1978), designed to investigate the presence and nature of infants' attachment.
- The study of Hazan and Shaver (1987) on adult styles of attachment relating to previous attachments made in infancy.
- The Rutter et al. (2001) investigation of the long-term effects of severe deprivation in childhood on attachment disorder.
- The work of Schoon and Bartley (2008) in means of building resilience to deprivation and adversity.

For identity development, look at the following:

- Hormone-based psychosexual differentiation theory, and the case study of David Reimer (Money, 1974).
- Gender-schema theory.
- The effect of social learning theory on gender roles (Bandura, 1977).
- Adolescent body image and identity: the cultural-ideal hypothesis (Symonds & Blyth, 1987).
- Erikson's theory of adolescent identity crisis.
- The investigation of Rutter et al (1976) on the reality of adolescent identity crisis.

SECTION ONE – COGNITIVE DEVELOPMENT

Evaluate theories of cognitive development *(for example, Piaget, Vygotsky, brain development theories).*

Reminder! 'Cognition refers to all those processes by which sensory input is transformed, reduced, elaborated, stored, recovered, and used... cognition is involved in anything a human being might possibly do' (Neisser, 1966). Human beings are regarded as information processors, and cognitivists explain behavior through these internal processes.

The development of current research in this area is inextricably linked with the biological perspective – especially the extremely complex brain function and neurological systems. This is the neurobiological approach to human development.

BRAIN DEVELOPMENT AND COGNITIVE FUNCTION: the work of Giedd (2004) involved a MRI-brain-scan-based longitudinal study of how the brain structure of healthy children develops with age. By the time the child reaches six, 95% of the brain structure is formed. However, the part of the brain that deals with the focus of attention, planning, and decision-making takes the longest to develop – typically becoming fully mature at around age 25.

THE EFFECT OF DEPRIVATION ON NEURO-PLASTICITY: brain plasticity is the brain's capacity to adapt to the challenges placed on it by developing appropriate new neurons which adapt the brain to the situation. For example you might find maths very difficult, but with regular practice, the part of the brain that deals with maths on a challenging basis 'thickens', and is able to handle maths more effectively. Thus the more your brain is exercised, the more powerful it becomes. In fact, every time we learn something new, the neurons connect to form a new trace in the brain. This is called **dendritic branching** because the branches (dendrites) of the neurons grow in numbers and connect with other neurons. (That is the biology of learning.)

The work of Perry (1997) compared the scans of brains of three-year-olds with normal degrees of human interaction with cases of those suffering extreme neglect – little experience of contact and interaction with other humans (such as observed in the infants adopted from Romanian orphanages in the 1990s). His finding were that (a) on the whole, the brains of severely neglected children tended to be smaller than those who had been normally nurtured, and (b) there were large ventricular spaces in the brains of the neglected children, which would negatively impact sleep, regulation of mood, and regulation of anxiety. He concluded that as a child grows, the brain absorbs all kinds of experiences. So if a child is not held, touched, talked to, and interacted-with, the neurons will cease to make enough connections to remain functional, and will simply die.

Indeed, **the work of Chugani et al. (2001)** on Romanian children who had spent time in orphanages before being adopted highlighted lack of development of the pre-frontal part of the brain, such as attention and social cognition. That is because there was a lack of socially-challenging stimulus to enable growth of that part of the brain through neuro-plasticity.

Overall, the biological approach to cognitive development holds that the brain develops along genetically-determined lines. It may be enhanced by positively stimulating social and environmental factors (brain plasticity). It may be undermined by a lack of stimulating social and environmental factors.

Strengths of neurobiological brain-development theories

   (a) Shows the connection between deprived social and environmental stimulation, and poorer brain development.
   (b) Provides evidence that suitable educational opportunities can biologically enhance brain development.

Limitations of neurobiological brain-development theories

   (a) Non-experimental nature of the studies makes it difficult to establish a direct relationship between brain neurobiological development and cognitive growth.
   (b) Brain scanning methods have not been used for long enough for complete longitudinal studies to be carried out on the same participant from birth to age 25.

PIAGET'S THEORY OF COGNITIVE DEVELOPMENT (1920s, and the decades until his death in 1980) predate modern brain-scanning methods.

Piaget's starting points in his theory of cognitive development are:

(a) Intellectual development occurs through active interaction with the world. Children do not passively receive their knowledge; they are curious and self-motivated. They are indeed experimenters.

(b) Intellectual development occurs as a process – children think in qualitatively different ways from adults – intelligence, knowledge, and understanding develop in stages. They cannot be pushed to function at higher stages of cognitive development before they have passed through the lower stages of cognitive development. And these stages of cognitive development are age-bound (as described below).

(c) The growing child builds increasingly complex schema – a unit of intelligent behavior that enables the individual to interact with and understand the world. For example, the infant is born with certain reflex actions, such as sucking or gripping. These schemas continue to develop and increase in their complexity (e.g. that gripping a rattle and gripping a cup are two different forms of gripping) and adapt the individual to function in the environment. The child builds the schema by experimenting. The child is thus an active partner in the early process.

Piaget's stages in his theory of cognitive development are:
- **Sensory-motor stage (ages 0-2)** – where the baby goes from reflex, instinctive actions (e.g. sucking a bottle) to constructing a knowledge by experience of what can be sucked and what cannot be sucked.
- **Pre-operational stage (ages 2-7)** – thinking is based on what the child sees, and from his/her point of view only. The child shows *egocentrism* (will not succeed in task where someone else is placed in a different part of the room, and the child has to describe what that person sees from his/her viewpoint), and *lack of conservation* (for example, if an adult pours water from a short wide glass into a narrow tall glass, the child will say that there is more water in that second glass because it is taller).
- **Concrete operational (7-11 years)** - needs to witness things carried out. The child will understand that there is the same amount of water in the tall glass on being seen the water being poured and glasses being handled.
- **Formal operational (12-15)** – can think abstractly, and work things out in the mind rather than have to reconstruct them physically. The older child can manipulate reasons, numbers, and ideas.

Strengths of Piaget's theories on child development

(a) It has demonstrated that children of different age groups process information differently, and certainly different from adults.
(b) It has placed emphasis on the teacher being a facilitator (to enable the child to learn through his or her own discoveries) rather than a disperser of knowledge.

Limitations of Piaget's theories of child development

(a) Child development may be seen as a continuous process rather than a series of stages.
(b) His research methods placed too much emphasis on deducing conclusions from the child's mistakes – to the degree that he may have overlooked abilities that children do possess, and may have wrongly deduced the reason for their failure.
(c) Neglected other cognitive factors that could have accounted for the individual differences in development, such as memory span, motivation, impulsiveness, practice, and linguistic ability.
(d) The child as an experimenter model seems to underestimate the importance of the involvement of adults and more knowledgeable peers.
(e) Vygotsky (1896-1934, see below), and Bruner (1915-fl.) argue that it is possible to speed up cognitive development provided that a suitable structure ('scaffolding') can be used to break down a complex topic and make it accessible to the child. This challenges the notion that teaching a child is only possible if he or she is within the appropriate stage of development.
(f) Knowledge of the biological functioning on the brain through brain-scanning techniques has advanced since Piaget's day.

VYGOTSKY'S SOCIO-CULTURAL APPROACH TO COGNITIVE DEVELOPMENT

Whilst agreeing with Piaget that the child's mind differs from the adult's, Vygotzky views language and instruction as the key factors of cognitive development. This is not just through creating the environment to promote the child discovering for him/herself (as Piaget). It is chiefly through cooperative interaction with the child in the instruction process.

It is the quality of contacts with more skilled individuals that counts in child development. Vygotsky identifies the **zone of proximal development** which is the area between what the child can do unaided (within the child's zone of competence) and what the child can achieve when 'stretched' by someone with more knowledge and skills.

This area is made accessible and achievable to the child by **scaffolding** (term introduced by Wood et. al. in 1986 as an extension of Vygotsky's zone of proximal development theory). That involves the instructor breaking down the new concept, skill, or task into suitably structured units through which the child can access the new areas, stage by stage.

Thus even a very young learner can master complex material so long as the material is appropriately scaffolded.

By extension, a child's development is a product of the framework of the instructors' (and indeed the society's) social and cultural norms.

Strengths of Vygotsky's theories on child development

(a) It puts forward the notion that children can handle more complex material than Piaget-age-appropriate – so long as it is suitably presented and broken down (scaffolded).
(b) It views child development from the continuous process of instruction and interaction, rather than from the outcomes expected at the end of each stage of cognitive development.
(c) It incorporates socio-cultural issues into the learning process and learning outcome.
(d) It also incorporates the linguistic ability and motivation of the child.

Limitations of Vygotsky's theories of child development

(a) Some lack of empirical support. His ideas are difficult to test as his emphasis is on the learning process rather than on the learning outcome.
(b) His heavy emphasis of the importance of social interaction in the child's development may be seen as underestimating fundamental biological issues.
(c) Knowledge of the biological functioning on the brain has advanced since Vygotsky's day, through brain-scanning techniques.

However, Vygotzky died when his work was in its infancy. Had he lived longer, he might have incorporated the criticisms of his work following peer review.

Discuss how social and environmental variables (for example, parenting, diet) may affect cognitive development.

One crucial social variable affecting cognitive development is parenting. It involves giving the child physical, emotional, social, and intellectual support, although in some societies this role may be partly given to older siblings.

The Michigan Department of Education (MDE) study (2002) found that the characteristics of home environments where children were doing well at school (in terms of enhanced cognitive development) included the following social family inputs:

(i) Well-established family routines – meals together, some child responsibility for household chores, set and well-established monitoring of TV viewing and bedtime.
(ii) Well-communicated values of self-discipline and hard work. Reading at home, listening to the child read, and discussing what has been read. [The work of Tizard (1982) shows that children who practice reading at home with their parents have a stronger tendency to progress faster in reading than those who read at school only.]
(iii) Good working relationships between the parents and the school. School activities are communicated by the parent as being means of enriching the child as a person and enabling preparation for better quality of life (including career-choice).

Applying Vygotsky, the factors above have enhanced cognitive development from an enriched zone of proximal development.

The work of Perry (1997) showed that good parenting enhanced cognition in terms of better physical brain development - neuroplasticity. The study compared the scans of brains of three-year-olds with normal degrees of human (very much including parental) interaction with cases of those suffering extreme neglect – little experience of contact and interaction with other humans (such as observed in the infants adopted from Romanian orphanages in the 1990s). His finding were that (a) on the whole, the brains of severely neglected children tended to be smaller than those who had been normally nurtured, and (b) there were large ventricular spaces in the brains of the neglected children, which would negatively impact sleep, regulation of mood, and regulation of anxiety. He concluded that as a child grows, the brain absorbs all kinds of experiences. So if a child is not held, touched, talked to, and interacted-with, the neurons will cease to make enough connections to remain functional, and will simply die.

Another crucial environmental variable affecting cognitive development is diet.

The work of Bhoomika (2008) studied the effects of malnourishment on the cognitive performance of two age-groups of Indian children: 5-7 and 8-10. Their data of cognitive achievement was compared with a control group of those who ate a regular diet. Those aged 5-7 showed less capacity to process information, in terms of processing information, memorizing, and visual-spatial tasks. Those aged 8-10 showed a smaller gap with the control group in these three areas, raising the possibility that poor diet delays rather than impairs cognitive development when other factors (such as an enriched zone of proximal development) are present.

The importance of eating breakfast on cognitive tasks at school was studied at the USA-based Food Research Action Center (2010), with those missing breakfast more likely to show poorer memory recall (don't forget breakfast before your exam), increased likelihood to make careless mistakes, and poorer results in cognitive tests. Indeed, as evidenced by the work of Raloff (1989) who studied 1023 sixth-grade students over one year, those given free school breakfasts substantially improved their scores for mathematics and sciences.

However, **Moscovici (1993)** emphasizes the importance of common sense in positive parenting. Children brought up in a well-disciplined and loving setting, given an optimal diet, and encouraged be reflective and set high goals for themselves, are likely to have higher self-esteem, higher-quality social relationships, and more likely to succeed in their chosen career in adulthood. Lack of one any one of those elements will not necessarily be the cause of substantial deterioration in cognitive development (see also Bhoomika, above).

SECTION TWO – SOCIAL DEVELOPMENT

Examine attachment in childhood and its role in the subsequent formation of relationships.

Attachment is a long-lasting, strong, and close emotional bond between two people. Separation causes suffering. The actual bond of attachment can be observed from the age of seven months. By that age infants become attached to specific people, and show distress when separated, Attachment theory is used to understand the social and emotional development of children, as well as adult relationships.

The presence of attachment or lack of attachment is the subject of the work of Ainsworth et al. (1978). Here, the research team tested how far a small child had been making an attachment by use of the 'Strange Situation' method. In this laboratory observation study, the mother and child were in an unfamiliar room and subjected to the 'strange situations' of a range of timed and increasingly stressful (for an attached child) set of scenarios such as: (i) a stranger is introduced to the child in the presence of the mother (ii) the mother leaves the infant with the stranger (iii) after the mother returns and re-settles the infant, it is left alone (iv) a stranger enters and interacts with the lone infant, and (v) the mother returns again and picks up the infant. Ainsworth discovered three main types of infant attachment using the Strange Situation: Type A – Detached or anxious-avoidant (20% of the sample of American infants) – the infant ignores the mother, is not affected by her parting, and although distressed when alone, is easily comforted by strangers. Type B – Securely attached (70% of the sample of American infants) – the infant plays contentedly when the mother is present, is distressed by her parting and although not adverse to stranger contact, treats them differently from the mother. Type C – Anxious-resistant or ambivalent (10% of the sample of American infants) – infant disconnected whilst with mother, playing less, is distressed with her parting, is not easily comforted on her return, and may resist contact by both the mother and the stranger.

In summary, three types of attachments – secure, ambivalent, and avoidant.

Indeed, Bowlby (1973) claims that there is development continuity. Early attachments with parents continue in later relationships, as the early attachments create an **internal working model**. That is a mental representation – a schema – about how one thinks about oneself, about how one thinks about the attachment figure, and about how others react. Where the child feels loved, he or she will tend to grow up with feelings of security, and will indeed feel worthy of love and attention. Where the child feels that the attachment figure is continually inaccessible, attachment-based disorders could be a problem later in life. Indeed, it is these early schemas that set the pattern for further attachments during infancy, childhood, adolescence, and finally adulthood.

The work of Hazan and Shaver (1978) sought to investigate the continuity theorized by Bowlby; that later relationships are influenced by attachments earlier in life. The study investigated how far attachment patterns in childhood were reflected in attachment styles in adulthood. Could 'different' attachment styles in adulthood be linked with the same 'different' attachment styles in childhood?

The investigation involved 620 participants responding to questionnaires. These were designed to elicit information about childhood relationship with parents (attachment history), and the nature of their most important adult relationship. The results were translated into an adaption of Ainsworth's categories of attachment, into adult styles of romantic love. These were (a) secure lovers (56%) who described their relationships as happy, trusting, and friendly (b) avoidant lovers (25%), who referred to their fears of intimacy, jealousies, and emotional roller-coasters, and (c) ambivalent lovers (19%), with periods of extreme sexual attraction, obsessions, and emotional roller coasters.

The results supported the Bowlby development continuity theory – that the child attachments highlighted in the 'strange situation' model do strongly influence attachment styles in adult personal relationships. The Hazan and Shaver study bridges the theories of infant attachment, and the theories of adult romantic love. It also indicates the importance of the main attachment figure (typically the mother) giving a great deal of her time and attention to interacting with the child in infancy in order to maximize good relationship-building capacities later in life.

The study has been criticized as the participants were a mostly female opportunist sample, recruited from responses volunteered in a newspaper survey. These people might well not have been representative of the general population.

Discuss potential effects of deprivation or trauma in childhood on later development.

Optimal child development tends to be a product of social and environmental factors, such as suitable parenting, being within proximal zones of positive stimulation, ideal diet, and relationships with a positive style of attachment.

A child is in deprivation where he or she is not having even basic needs taken care of – whether physical, emotional, or social.

A child suffers trauma where there is a powerful shock: death of parents, divorce, serious abuse, or war and refugee status. Deprivation experiences can also create trauma for the child.

Deprivation and trauma can impair the child's development. However, not all children suffer permanent damage. Some eventually develop normally (see below).

The work of Rutter et al. (2004) sought to investigate the long-term effects of severe deprivation in childhood on (a) cognitive development and (b) attachment disorder.

The study investigated a sample of 144 adopted children aged six years old. They were in two groups. The first were from UK institutions who had been subsequently adopted. The second were severely-deprived children from Romanian institutions, who had been subsequently adopted in the UK. In some cases, the children had spent their first three-and-a-half years there.

It was the long-term effects of their deprivation on reaching the age of six that was the focus of the study. By that time, they had already spent more than two years (at least) in their adoptive families in the UK.

Information from the adoptive parents on the family and the child's behavior patterns was obtained by parent interviews and questionnaires. Three months later, the researchers observed the adopted children, and gave them standard tests for cognitive impairment and attachment disorder.

For attachment disorder, the focus was on the behavior of the children towards the adoptive parents in both familiar and 'strange' situations (Ainsworth-type scenarios). The attachment disorders found included (i) no special preference for the adoptive parent over any other adults, and (ii) not turning to the adoptive parent for help in an anxiety situation.

With cognitive impairment, the results showed no significant trends with children that suffered less than six months deprivation in Romanian institutions. There was significant cognitive impairment in 12% of the children who had been there from between six months and two years. That figure went up to 36% for those between two years and three-and-a-half years. That was particularly significant for those who had additionally suffered severe malnutrition before adoption. In addition, children who had remained a long time in the Romanian deprived orphanages had a significantly smaller head circumference, suggesting neural damage.

With attachment disorder, the results were fairly similar. Again, no significant trend of cognitive impairment was found with children having been less than six months in Romanian institutions. There was significant attachment disorder in 16% of the children who had been there from between six months and two years. That figure went up to 33% for those between two years and three-and-a-half years. This suggests that lack of suitable, individualized child rearing puts the child's cognitive and social development at risk.

However, by the age of six, most children showed neither cognitive impairments nor attachment disorders. This indicates that the effects of severe-deprived child-rearing are not necessarily irreversible, indicating some degree of resilience, as below.

Define resilience.

Resilience is the person's capacity to 'bounce back' from past traumatic events and situations. It is, as Rutter (1990) puts it, maintaining adaptive functioning in spite of having been exposed to risk factors.

Risk factors include poverty, family breakdown, and death of a close relative. These may be offset by protective factors, such as individual care-giving, and opportunities to develop feelings of self-worth.

The work of Schoon and Bartley (2008) indicates that adaptive personality traits help, but not everyone has the resources to 'bounce back' through their own efforts.

Discuss strategies to build resilience.

The environment can create optimum conditions for the development of resilience-building capacities. These include inputs from schools, peer counseling, individual counseling, play counseling, home-visit programs, and after-school programs in high-risk communities.

Schools have the capacity to develop resilience capacities given that they accept the ideal that they are not just dispensers of academic information, but sources of personal values, development of aspirations, contact with ideal role models, and creators of realizable expectations beyond the walls of the classroom. Not all schools meet that ideal, or even have the resources to achieve that ideal.

Strategy of enhancing resilience development: the work of Sagor (1996), and Wang et al. (1994) indicates that schools may indeed support resilience-development with high-risk children through programs that enable them to feel that they are able to succeed at a task. Schools also need to communicate to those children that they 'belong', that they are valued in the school community, and that they can indeed make a difference. The school should exercise the capacity to create/maintain a general atmosphere of forward-looking optimism.

In practice, struggling schools in deprived areas will have greater difficulties in being able to create such an atmosphere. There is also the issue of being able to exercise suitable supervision where already at-risk children are most likely to face further adversity, such as during movements between lessons, and in the playground.

Strategy of enhancing coping skills: the New York Center for Children suggests the following strategies to develop children's coping skills improve their resilience. Children at risk cannot be expected to do that for themselves. The New York Center for Children emphasizes that children's improved coping skills may be developed by **enabling parents to progress in their child-rearing skills,** including:

(a) Home-visits programs – to enhance the level of attachment between mother and baby, helping the mother to cope with her own issues of poverty, lack of access to healthcare, and maternal depression.
(b) Teenage parent support and training – to empower such mothers to cope with the reality of child rearing, reaching out to members of the extended family for child care, and enabling where possible for the mother to complete her high-school studies and graduate. Such programs also involve group therapy, where teenage mothers give support to each other, therefore reducing their feelings of loneliness and helplessness.
(c) Early Head Start programs for all children and families – involving parental-skills training programs. The work of Love et al. (2005) indicates that those parents who participated in those programs progressed substantially in stimulating their children's language development, and improved their emotional-support skills.
(d) After-school programs in high-risk communities – supported by the work of Mahoney (2005) whose longitudinal study showed that children who had attended those programs for as little as one year showed substantial improvement in motivation, reading skills, and test results.

The difficulties involved include the additional expense of providing services to the child rather than just information to the parents, and to the schools. In addition, New York City is a very multi-racial society. Not all minority groups feel comfortable at having their communities being entered with those objectives.

SECTION THREE – IDENTITY DEVELOPMENT

Discuss the formation and development of gender roles.

Gender roles characterize activities as being male or female. Gender roles are sets of behaviors associated with being male or female. These set the ways males and females behave in specific situations and socio-cultural settings.

Psychologists debate the degree that the differences between males and females are due to innate biological differences on one hand, and socialization differences on the other. Specifically, does a boy follow the masculine stereotype because that is within his hormonal structure, or because he was brought up that way?

Each contributor to the gender role is considered separately.

Biologically-based theories of gender role include evolutionary theory, and hormone-based psychosexual differentiation theory.

Evolutionary theory explains gender roles having formed and developed out of the needs of early societies. Men were required to be tough and competitive: in attracting a female partner, and in due course being able to obtain the scarce resources for their children. Women focused on nurturing themselves in order to attract a quality male. They continued as nurturers of the children, leaving the men to continue to compete in bringing home quality resources.

Hormone-based psychosexual differentiation theory focuses on gender roles being formed and developed by biological determination. Androgens such as testosterone are what make a male feel male. They are seen as having a masculinizing effect on the way the developing male mentally processes information. Socialization is only of secondary importance. According to this theory, children are *not* born psychologically-gender-neutral and then socialized into their gender role.

This is supported by findings from the David Reimer case (Money, 1974). This is a longitudinal case study which appears to have supported the biological school. *The facts of the case were that Bruce Reimer, an identical twin, had his penis accidentally cut off at the age of 8 months during a routine circumcision. Psychologist John Money successfully persuaded the parents to change Bruce's gender through surgery and hormone-replacement. The child was renamed Brenda, and raised as a girl. This was a unique opportunity for Money to test his belief that children were gender neutral and could be raised according to the norms of either gender. Brenda's twin brother was an ideal control. Money published articles showing that gender roles could be bio-socially determined, but he left out the evidence that went against his theory. Brenda had become increasingly unhappy with the other girls, and also at her sessions with Money. At age 15, Brenda's parents told her the truth. Brenda decided to become a male again, and went through the appropriate surgery to restore his gender, renaming himself David. He subsequently married at age 22.*

This case study appears to support the notion that hormone-based psychosexual differentiation theory dominates gender roles. These fundamental gender roles cannot readily be bio-socially changed. It has the limitations inherent to being a single case study.

Cognitive-based theories of gender role include gender-schema theory

Gender schemas are rooted in society's beliefs about how boys and girls are expected to behave. Children form and develop their gender roles as they receive affirming and disapproving feedback to the degree that they tend to conform to the behavior accepted of their gender. Boys to action-men, girls to dolls – not the other way round. These schemas influence the way the child processes subsequent information. They also influence the child's self-esteem, where behavior consistent with the schema-generated gender role receives the approval of those around the child.

Gender schemas can determine what and what will not be of interest to the child: boys to football, girls to caring activities. They also influence who they would like to sit next to in class, and be friends with – the work of Fagot (1985) based on observation indicated that at the age of two, boys made fun of boys who played with dolls, or with girls. And even at that age, girls were not too happy with the girls who played with boys. This was also the case with the older 10-11 year-old age group. The work of Sroufe et al. (1993) found that those that did not behave according to their gender-stereotype were the least popular.

These studies indicate that peer-pressure (social element) reinforces the gender-stereotype, and thus the gender schema (cognitive element).

Gender schemas can determine how boys and girls process the same information: the work of Martin & Halvorson (1983) showed a group of 5-6 year-old some pictures of children's activities. Some were in line with the gender role (e.g. a boy playing with a gun), and some went against the gender role (e.g. a girl playing with a gun). The children's recall was tested a week later. Those scenes with out-of-gender roles tended to be remembered incorrectly (for example the picture of a girl playing with a gun was recalled as a boy playing with a gun. For that example was outside the framework of the gender schema.

However, the gender schemas have the limitations of tending to focus on the individual experience, and not the more general socialization processes and cultural issues.

Social theories of gender role include social learning theory (Bandura, 1977).

Social learning theory suggests that gender roles are learnt and developed out of interactions with the environment and modeling those of the same gender. This involves the **observation** of same-sex people, which may lead to **imitation** if the behavior to be copied appears to lead to desirable consequences.

It involves paying attention to the person modeled, remembering the behavior that was observed, subsequently replicating the action, and feeling good about demonstrating what has been learnt. It is distinguished from conditioning, in that the learning is indirect (not stimulus/response/reward). It models the behavior of others (vicarious learning), and gets reinforcement according to the results of following that behavior.

Indeed, social learning theory in the form of **peer-socialization** may well explain the finding of Fagot (1985) which indicated that at the age of two, boys made fun of boys who played with dolls, or with girls. And even at that age, girls were not too happy with the girls who played with boys. This was also the case with the older 10-11 year-old age group. The work of Sroufe et al. (1993) found that those that did not behave according to their gender-stereotype were the least popular.

However, social learning theory does not explain why there is a considerable variation in conformity to gender stereotypes among boys and girls.

Explain cultural variations in gender roles.

Cultural elements refer to distinctive beliefs, values, and practices within a specific group that are passed down from one generation to the next.

Cultural differences appear to modify the biological determinism view, which would make gender roles and behaviors universal, which is not the case in all cultures.

The work of anthropologist Margaret Mead (1935) compared the gender roles in three tribes in New Guinea.

The Arapesh Tribe – both genders cooperated in work and child-rearing, in a peaceful manner.

The Mundugumor Tribe – both genders followed the male stereotype of being aggressive, arrogant, and competitive. Women were not interested in child rearing, and the child who left parental care at the earliest possible opportunity was a status symbol.

The Tchambuli Tribe – women did the hard work to sustain the family, whilst men idled trying to look good, and chat to other men.

Her argument, based on the differences between the three tribes below, is that gender roles are culturally-based rather than biologically-based.

Echoes of Meade's argument have been found in the following studies:

(a) **Engle and Breaux (1994)** found that fathers have become more involved in child-rearing where they have participated in parenting and child-development programs.

(b) **Reinicke (2006)** found that young fathers in Denmark actually view their fathering, child-rearing roles as part of their personal identity. *Indeed, it may be argued that this may become closer to the norm in individualist, Western society as social equality is increasingly taken for granted. It can also be linked with women's greater control over wealth and resources.*

Describe adolescence.

Adolescence is the development period between puberty and adulthood. The age of reaching sexual maturity is too early to acquire the skills and assume the responsibilities to function in complex Western society. In contrast to many traditional societies with their out-of-childhood initiation ceremonies, Western society does not have any formal transition markers. Thus the age boundaries of adolescence vary, but are typically between 11 and 21.

In an exam, you may be required to examine adolescence in detail. Include physical and cognitive changes and features of adolescence as relevant to the terms of the question.

Discuss the relationship between physical change and development of identity during adolescence.

Physical changes in adolescence include:

(i) An upsurge in sex-hormones: including testosterone (for boys), oestrogen (for girls).
(ii) Physical growth spurts. With boys, there is also voice deepening, broadening of the shoulders, development of more powerful muscles, and facial/genital hair growth. With girls: development of breasts, widening of the hips, and gain in weight.
(iii) Sexual maturation typically takes place about two years earlier in girls than in boys.

Developmental psychology considers how adolescent physical changes influence the personal identity of boys and girls.

Sexual identity – focuses on the reality that adolescents accept themselves as sexually mature, but they are not likely to be in a socially-recognized permanent sexual relationship. Sexual urges and activities become real issues. Those living in some cultures have to come to terms with the fact that sexual exploration is unacceptable. They may evolve coping strategies that accept their sexuality without being able to exercise it. In other cultures, sexual exploration is seen as evidence of normal behavior, though even the more liberal framework can create issues with those whose sexual identity is on same-sex relationships. Additionally, girls have to deal with the notion that their sexual awareness and attractiveness can send out messages that are responded to with inappropriate male attentions and dangers of sexual violence.

Body image and identity: the cultural-ideal hypothesis (Symonds & Blyth, 1987) suggest that puberty brings boys closer to their ideal body image, whereas it takes girls further from theirs.

On the whole, boys like their fast maturing bodies and are only disappointed when they feel that their physical development is not as fast as the rest of their crowd. As long as they are getting big and strong, all is OK.

Girls in early and mid-adolescence do not welcome physical changes where they clash with their ideal of having a slim body – an ideal reinforced by socialization and the media.

Cultural differences: the work of Ferron (1997) compared the way French adolescents and American adolescents identified with their physical developments. Using samples of 60 male and female adolescents from each culture, they interviewed each participant to elicit the way they perceived their body changes, and how they coped with them. Three-quarters of the Americans were not satisfied with their physical appearance, but more than three-quarters believed that they could achieve their ideal body shape with suitable dieting and exercise. Thus the Americans seemed more likely to feel intense self-guilt when their body shapes did not match their ideals.

The French were also overall dissatisfied with their physical shape, but less than half of the sample believed that it was in their power to reach their ideal. The best that could be done was to take great care of the physique that they had. Unlike three-quarters of the American girls, they did not tend to assess their self-worth in terms of their slimness.

However: this cognitive study may be criticized for the small-size of the sample, and the reliance on the self-reporting within the interview. It could also have been that the French adolescents were less inclined to full self-disclosure at interview.

Examine psychological research into adolescence *(for example, Erikson's identity crisis.).*

"I ain't what I ought to be, I ain't what I'm gonna be, but I ain't what I was" (Erikson 1950, in describing the **identity crisis that goes with adolescence**).

Erikson divides the human-life cycle into eight phases of psychosocial development. Each phase involves a challenge, and successful living involves meeting the challenges of each phase positively and successfully. He argues that adolescents find it difficult to find their identity because of the physical changes that they are experiencing. In short, **identity versus confusion**. Typically, phases of low self-esteem and low productivity.

If in time the adolescent overcomes the identity crisis successfully, he or she is ready to progress into adulthood. **However, the actual identity crisis can involve the following:**

(a) Not knowing who you are and who you are about to become – role confusion.
(b) Ambivalence over facing changes (sexual, future careers, eventually settling down) that are taking place, and feeling that things will not quite be the same as they were.
(c) Possible phase of negative identity – scorning the family and home culture, maybe joining a subculture with a socially unacceptable identity.
(d) Difficulty in coping with one's demands in a balanced manner. There can be a tendency to put everything off and go into a temporary suspension of activity, with the need of 'finding yourself' (what Erikson calls a **psychosocial moratorium** – something not accommodated in all societies), or alternatively to put a massive amount of energy into one activity.

Erikson's theoretical framework for tackling adolescence is based on observing individual adolescents in therapy in the 1940s and 1950s, which means that it should be used with caution when applying to a wider group.

The work of Rutter et al (1976) aimed to investigate whether or not Erikson's developmental identity crisis was indeed typical of adolescents. It was conducted on the Isle of Wight, UK, and involved the participation of every 14-15 year old on the island (a total of

2,303). Data came from questionnaire surveys, and interviews with teachers, parents, and adolescents.

The results of this cohort study (so called as it did not involve a sample, but everyone in the target population) showed that less than one quarter of the teenagers showed identity crisis characteristics or conflict with parents, and much of that was traceable to other psychological problems. It seemed that the Erikson stage of conflict was by no means universal amongst adolescents.

This study had the strengths of being a cohort rather than a sample study, and the interviews with parents and teachers overall supported the adolescents' reporting. It may be criticized as it interviewed students that were youngish adolescents, some of whom may not yet have reached the identity crisis stage. In addition, there may be problems with self-reported data – the students not wishing to report what they secretly felt, but were not prepared to confide to their parents or teachers.

It may be argued that Erikson's theory is less valid today as society accommodates and encourages more gradual merging into adult life-styles. Career preparation is a longer process, changing professions is becoming more common and acceptable, and the average age of marriage has risen.

POSSIBLE EXAMINATION QUESTIONS

LONG ANSWER QUESTIONS ONLY ON PAPER TWO

(a) Define resilience.
(b) Discuss strategies to build resilience.

Evaluate any two theories of cognitive development.

Discuss any two theories for the development of gender roles.

CHAPTER SIX – HEALTH PSYCHOLOGY

Paper 2 – option topic

Remember that you are applying the biological, cognitive, and socio-cultural perspectives to specific issues within the field of health psychology.

Health psychology looks at how issues such as stress, substance abuse, addiction, obesity, and health promotion may impact on a person's physical well-being.

The goal of health psychology is to enable the healthy to stay as healthy for as long as possible, and for those with health-issues (obesity, alcoholism, stress, smoking, drug-addiction) to commence and adhere to suitable treatments.

Learning outcomes of this unit: General framework (applicable to all topics in the option)

To what extent do biological, cognitive and socio-cultural factors influence health-related behavior?

For biological influences, look at the following below:

- General adaptation system in coping with stress.
- The effects of stress in lowering resistance to disease – the experimental work of Kiecolt-Glaser et al.
- The study of Difranza on addiction to smoking.
- The study of Stunkard on the role of genes in overeating-caused obesity.

For cognitive influences, look at the following below:

- The study of Sarafino on stress in the workplace, based on the perceived gap between the demands of a situation and what people think they are able to do.
- The study of Speisman on how one's interpretation of an event rather than the actual event affects arousal and stress.
- The study of Charlton on how smoking might be encouraged by positive images in the media.
- The health-belief model in health promotion.

For socio-cultural influences, look at the following below:

- The work of Evans and Kim in investigating the long-term relationship between the social condition of poverty and its associated chronic stressors.
- The role of social support as a means of coping with stress.
- The stages of change model in health promotion, and the work of West and Sohal.

Evaluate psychological research (that is, theories and/or studies) relevant to health psychology.

For stress, look at the following:

- General adaptation system in coping with stress.

- The effects of stress in lowering resistance to disease – the experimental work of Kiecolt-Glaser et al.
- The study of Speisman on how one's interpretation of an event rather than the actual event affects arousal and stress.

For substance abuse, addictive behavior and obesity, look at the following

- The value of social support, and MSBR (mindfulness stress reduction) in coping with stress, and cutting smoking and obesity-promoting habits.
- The value of CBT (cognitive behavior therapy)

Health promotion, look at the following:

- The health-belief model in health promotion, and the work of Quist-Paulsen and Gallefors.
- The stages of change model in health promotion, and the work of West and Sohal.

SECTION ONE – STRESS

Describe stressors.

Stress is the failure to respond appropriately to physical and emotional threats. These threats may be real ones or imagined ones – the symptoms are the same.

Stress-based reactions might be *physiological* (e.g. Gross 1996 argues that people catch colds soon after high-stress events, for example exams), *cognitive* (such as some people's fear of dogs), and *behavioral* (men typically like to whack a punch-bag to work off stress, whereas women prefer to telephone and chat to a friend).

Stressors are typically felt by quickening pulse, pounding heart, sweating hands, and 'butterflies' in the stomach (all physical responses to a new or threatening situation). Stressors range from factors such as noise, pain, violence, working conditions, giving up smoking, and exams.

Stressors (causes of stress) vary from person to person. For example, some people revel in public speaking and even get 'high' on it. Others might be more scared of making an after-dinner speech than parachuting with a free-fall from an aircraft. Muhammad Ali (aka Cassius Clay), twice world heavyweight boxing champion, was known to get tongue-tied in asking a woman for a date! Those in high-stress occupations include business administrators, air-traffic controllers, surgeons, and school-teachers.

Acute stressors – appear immediately, do not last long, and call for immediate attention, such as a sports injury or the attack of a predator.

Acute minor stress typically might include: you are left out of a game during recess, you get a large pimple on your forehead, or you receive a poor grade for a long-answer essay test in psychology after a hard weekend's preparation.

Acute major Stress could involve your moving with your family to a new town and have to enter school in the middle of the year. Or being hit by a car when out on your bike and seeing your front four teeth on the ground.

Chronic stressors last for a long time and a constant source of worry.

Chronic minor Stress may come from your feelings of having to babysit your little brother every Friday after school. Or having to sit in your disliked assigned seat during psychology class. Every single psychology class, that is.

Chronic major stress could be rooted in your parents working long hours and being never home. Or there is too much going on. Everyone – your parents, your teachers, your friends, are demanding at the same. All the time. (And nobody says thank you.)

Chronic stressors are generally more dangerous than acute stressors for the following reason. In acute stress, the body will temporarily go into a state of alert and deal with the stress with inputs from the nervous and endocrine systems. Once that acute stress has passed, the body returns to homeostasis (balance between external environment and the body's normal physiological state). But in chronic stress, the body does not return to homeostasis, because the stressor (whether real or imagined) is constantly there.

The degree of stress suffered depends to a great extent on the person's personality type. If the person is a Type A, s/he is driven urgently towards achievements and success in competition (in contrast to the more easily-paced Type B personality). Type As will run rather than walk up the moving staircase, and will be impatient in long lines at the supermarket checkout. The Type C personality appear to be more laid back (as in Type B), but is being driven by Type A forces. Unlike Type A, s/he will bottle the force rather than express it in impatience, aggression, and hostility when confronting roadblocks to progress. Both Type As and Cs are more prone to suffer from stress, rather than Type Bs.

Stress in the workplace generally arises where there is a mismatch between the demands made on a person and his/her ability to cope with them – for example lack of control on how to handle a job (e.g. an under-confident teacher), and tightness of deadlines.

Some of the main work stressors that have been identified by the UK National Work-Stress Network include: working under constant deadlines, no recognition or reward for good job performance, harassment or bullying at work, and shifting goalposts from new management techniques and new technology.

Frequent workplace stress is caused by a mismatch between what the worker can do, and the set task. It can also be because of poor leadership at the top, and poor communication of what has to be done. Worker stress can occur on perceiving a gap between the demands of a situation and what you feel you are able to do. ('I can't handle it') As far as stress is concerned, whether this gap is realistic or unrealistic makes no difference.

Changes in daily routine can be stressful – even if positive, such as getting married, or getting the long-awaited job promotion (as below).

To measure stress on the Holmes and Rahe Stress Scale (1967 – based on an opportunist sample of around 400 people in the USA), the number of 'Life Change Units' that apply to events in the past year of an individual's life are added, and the final score estimates how stress affects health.

The scale was devised in the following way. Participants were given a very wide range of stressful events, and they ticked off those of which they had recent experience. They then rated the events in terms of how long they thought it would take to readjust and accommodate the stressor. The researchers found a very high degree of correlation between the respondents. Further tests showed a fairly constant result among Hispanic, African, and white people within the USA. The scale was also tested cross-culturally and revealed similar results – comparing Japanese and Malaysian groups with the USA population.

The maximum stressor score went to the most stressful event normally occurring in life – death of a spouse (100). Divorce came in at 73, marriage at 50, dismissal from work at 47, outstanding personal achievement at 28, and Christmas, 12. The higher the score, the greater the stress, with a 12-month-accumulated 150 points being a candidate for stress-related illness, and a score of 300 being a high risk for stress-related illness.

Discuss physiological, psychological and social aspects of stress

Physiological (biological) aspects of stress

Physiologically (biologically), the sympathetic nervous system and endocrine system prepare the individual to either confront (fright, fight) or run away (fright, flight) from the source of stress. These systems combine. Through increased levels of adrenaline, they increase blood pressure and glucose levels in the muscles. These energize the body to confront or quickly get away from the threat.

Selye's (1956) experimentation with stressors on laboratory rats suggests that they (and humans) have a dealing-with-stress mechanism called the **general adaptation syndrome (GAS)**. The body reacts in three phases to a stressor (see diagram). In the first phase – **alarm** – the body mobilizes to confront the threat which temporarily expands resources to cope – fright/flight/fight. The stress brings an initial lowering of resistance (feeling of shock), but then gains in resistance to confront the stressor. In the second stage – the **resistance** stage – the body is actively coping/resisting on a much higher than the normal level of functioning, and at the same time reversing the effects of the alarm stage – coping with the stressor without the initial lack of confidence. The third stage is **exhaustion** – after prolonged coping with stressors, the body is no longer able to cope any further.

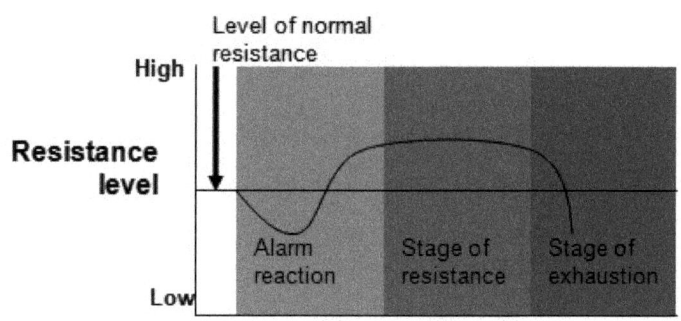

Stages of syndrome

Many students report that they cannot write their exam response in the first few minutes even if they know their material and can apply it to the question. (The five-minute reading time that the IB gives you should help you to handle that one.) After that, they go up to a 'high' and write a much better answer than if they were doing it at home in their own study. Once the exam is over – collapse!

Strengths of GAS:
(a) It explains the fatigue that people suffer after prolonged stress – like your struggle to get back to the changing room after a particularly exciting soccer match.
(b) It does help to account for the interaction of environmental (as opposed to organic) stressors and physiological (biological) responses.

Weaknesses of GAS
(a) It focuses on fight/fright/flight. It does not readily accommodate the use of other methods of dealing with stress (such as whacking a punchbag, telephoning a friend).
(b) It does not readily account for how people suffer stress by merely thinking about stressful events.

The effects of stress in lowering resistance to disease – the experimental work of Kiecolt-Glaser et al (1984) looked at the T-cell (immune system, fight disease) count in a group of medical students one month (control), and then the day before their final examinations (test). The students also completed scales of life events, bodily symptoms, and levels of satisfactions with interpersonal contacts. The researchers found that the second blood sample taken on the day before revealed a lower T-cell count. So did the counts from students with a higher level of stressful events and loneliness. This indicates that psychological stress influences the immune system.

Since then, psychologists have become aware that long-term stress causes an increase in **cortisol**, which not only leads to depression and memory problems, but a decrease in the number of T-cells that cause the immune system to weaken.

Strengths:
(a) The experiment was longitudinal. The same people were the source of data for the control and test situation.
(b) The experiment was part of the medical students' real-life situation, and therefore ecologically valid.

Weaknesses:
(a) As it was a 'natural' experiment and not in laboratory conditions, it was difficult to establish cause and effect.
(b) The lower T-cell count could have been a result of something else that all the students had gone through that was not connected with the questionnaire (above). It might not have been directly connected with stressors.

Psychological (cognitive) aspects of stress

The cognitive approach is based on their being a link between one's psychological state (e.g. optimism or pessimism), and the efficacy of the immune system - via the nervous system. This is approach is called psychoneuroimmunology (PNI).

The transactional model of stress and coping cognitive appraisal model (following Lazarus & Folkman, 1984) emphasizes how people confront new stressful situations in two stages. In the first appraisal, they interpret what they sense as positive or negative. In the second appraisal, they consider which coping strategy to apply in coping with the stressor.

The interpretation of an event affects the degree of arousal and stress. In the experimental work of Speisman et al (1964), the participants were divided into three groups. All were shown the same unpleasant movie, featuring the details of the ceremony of tribal genital mutilation. Each group, however, heard a different soundtrack. The first group heard the trauma situation – with emphasis on the pain and the mutilation. The second heard the denial situation – where the tribes-people appeared to be gratified by what was going on. And the third heard a commentary giving an anthropological description of the ceremony.

The researchers compared the stress responses of the three groups, all of whom had viewed the same material. Those who heard the trauma situation showed more significant stress responses that the other two groups - in terms of increased heartbeat, skin response, and in their answers to the post-experiment questionnaires. This seems to indicate that cognitive appraisal (as later described by Lazarus & Folkman) has a significant role in determining which biological strategies are used in addressing the stressor.

Strengths:
(a) Seems to support the theory that it is not the stressor, but the appraisals of the stressor that creates the reactions.

(b) The laboratory setting made it easier to control cause (appraisal) and effect (stress reactions).

Weaknesses:
(a) The experiment was in a strictly laboratory environment, raising issues of ecological validity.
(b) The deception used and the anxiety experienced by the participants in the trauma situation would need justification by today's ethical standards.

The interpretation of a person's own situation affects the degree of arousal and stress. The work of Reed et al. (1999) showed that HIV-positive people with more pessimistic expectations develop HIV-related symptoms more easily. Kemeny et. al (2006) took it further, showing that pessimistic expectations may simply lead to people giving up – which by itself weakens the immune system. This also implies that optimism in interpreting the HIV-positive situation can help the person to survive for a longer period.

Overall, this perspective provides some scientific basis of positive thinking for good health, but there is currently insufficient empirical evidence for generalized conclusions.

Social aspects of stress

Given that people require the company of others for psychological well-being, stressful social relationships may threaten that well-being. This includes difficulties with spouse, between members of the (dysfunctional, non-supported, conflict-ridden) family, and in the school, workplace, or neighborhood.

Conversely, those coming from families that are functional, warm, and supportive are likely to develop the necessary social skills enhancing positive social interactions. The work of Smith et al. (1992) found that adults whose interpersonal interactions were hostile and cynical were less likely to feel socially-supported.

The work of Evans and Kim (2007) aimed to investigate the long-term relationship between the social condition of poverty and its associated chronic stressors, and the degree of physiological stress suffered in the long term.

Two hundred seven-year-olds from backgrounds of poverty took part in the study. The investigation used a standard acute stressor: measuring the degree that the heart reacted to the stressor, and how long it took for the heartbeat to return to the normal level. The result was that the more time spent in poverty, the higher the cortisol level and the longer it took for heartbeat to return to normal. The researchers concluded that exposure to poor physical and social living conditions build up chronic stress. That accumulation of chronic stressors creates higher risks of long-term negative effects on both physical and mental health.

Evaluate strategies for coping with stress.

Stress-coping strategy #1 – Social Support

This may be defined as the experience that comes of knowing that one is part of a social network of family or friends, and believing that others do care about you. This support may be **practical** (tangible, e.g. financial assistance), **emotional** (warmth and understanding), and **informational** (helping a person to cope better with a stressful situation). This is supported by the following studies:

(a) The work of Belle (1987) found that **adult women maintained more same-sex close friends** and received more social support in times of stress than men.

(b) There appear to be **gender-differences in the nature of support offered**. For example the work of Klemm (1999), which performed a content-analysis of postings on various Internet-based cancer-support groups – including breast and prostate cancer. It found that the most common posting on the web-pages were seeking and giving information, encouragement, and support. Women were more than twice as likely as men to provide encouragement and support, and men were more than twice as likely to offer information.

(c) There appear to be **cultural differences in the implications of seeking social support** as a coping strategy. The work of Taylor (2004) explored the differences in this practice between European, US, and Korean students. They found that a significantly lower number of Korean students used social support as a means of coping. They suggested that this was a reflection of the Asian concern of disruption of harmony in the group, social criticism, or losing face, as opposed to Western culture's emphasis on the well-being of the individual as an independent unit.

(d) The increasing popularity of **stress-related Internet groups** seems to indicate their efficacy in helping people. This is supported by the work of Wenzelberg et al. (2003), which evaluated the beneficial effects of online support groups. The participants were a controlled group of 72 women diagnosed with breast cancer. As a controlled experiment, some of them were randomly assigned to a 12-week web-based social-support group. The participants were told specifically that the group was psycho-educational, rather than psychotherapeutic. The researchers found that indeed the Internet-based programs were moderately effective in reducing participants' scores on perceived stresses and depression.

However, these researchers argue that studies based on web-based support groups contain ethical issues of participant confidentiality, and possible deception in not understanding the role of the facilitator (psycho-educational rather than psychotherapeutic).

Stress-coping strategy #2 – Mindfulness stress reduction (MSBR)

This may be defined as responding to the stress situation in a mentally-proactive manner, rather than reacting to it automatically. With repeated practice, the individual develops the ability to **step back calmly from thoughts and feelings during stressful situations toward proactive coping strategy**, rather than negative thinking patterns that may escalate various stress responses.

The repeated practice may take several forms. It can include bodily scan (meditation practice – usually performed lying down, with the eyes closed – then direct attention to different parts of the body in turn – and focusing and accepting whatever sensation comes from each part). It can also include yoga exercises, where participants become aware of the body's different sensations, including those of tension and relaxation. It may include sitting meditation – uptight but relaxed posture, and focus on the physical sensation of breathing. The participant allows the mind to wander when it happens, but returns the mind to breathing once more.

The participants are encouraged to bring mindfulness to their everyday lives. For example, when showering, the person is required to focus on the present moment, noticing the sensations experienced whilst doing it as in meditation.

MSBR's overall efficacy may be gauged by looking at – the work of Shapiro et al. (1998) on a controlled sample of pre-medical students in the University of Arizona. As participation, they enrolled on the MSBR course, for three credits. Based on self-reporting questionnaires at the beginning of the course, and just before the medical exams (a high stress period), those doing the course did not differ from the control group not doing the course at the beginning of the semester, but did experience significant differences at the time of the exams. This suggests that course had enabled them to cope effectively with the exams. It may be criticized on the ground of being based entirely on medical students – and their being offered course credits for having participated.

SECTION TWO – SUBSTANCE ABUSE, ADDICTIVE BEHAVIOR, AND OBESITY

Explain factors related to the development of substance abuse or addictive behavior (our example is smoking and nicotine).

- A substance in this context is something that is ingested to alter mood, cognition, or behavior – e.g. nicotine.
- Addiction is where there is a compulsion to use the substance in order to avoid discomfort in its absence – e.g. craving for a cigarette. A smoker who cannot quit despite wanting to do so is an addict.
- Substance addiction may be psychological – certain situations might serve as triggers for the craving for a smoke, such as after a meal, on the phone, or when feeling stressed.
- Substance addiction may be physiological – with a greater amount to produce the same effect (tolerance), and withdrawal symptoms if the substance is not taken.

Biological factors related to addictive behavior – smoking

(a) Hormones and neurotransmitters - nicotine has the effect of stimulating (hormone) adrenaline release. This puts strain on the heart, raises blood pressure, and releases (neurotransmitter) dopamine with its accompanying feelings of pleasure. Nicotine acts on acetylcholine neurotransmitters as though it was the natural neurotransmitter, creating more acetylcholine receptors sites in the process. Withdrawal means that these new receptor sites are yearning for neurotransmitters, resulting in a craving for more cigarettes. This makes it difficult for smokers to give up, which in the USA has been estimated at being 80% of its smoking population.

(b) Immediate pleasure: the study of Difranza et al (2006) showed that young adolescents who had an immediate positive, relaxing experience at the first puff are nearly three times as likely to get addicted as those who did not get such an effect. Indeed, two-thirds of those who enjoyed their first puff went on to become addicts. Thus Difranza highlights that the likelihood of getting addicted depends on the individual. It also highlights the dangers of trying to smoke – even once. What was not determined was why some people were able to smoke without becoming addicted, which is argued to be a combination of genetic and environmental factors.

Cognitive factors related to addictive behavior – smoking

Cognitively – the study of Charlton (1984) showed that young smokers associated smoking with fun and pleasure (cognitive argument). Today the focus of cigarette advertizing is in developing countries such as China, where despite poverty, two-thirds of the male population were smokers in 2001. With approximately a third of Chinese teenagers being smokers, the advertizing continues, promoting the association of smoking with independence and sex appeal. Charlton also found that those who demonstrated a strong interest in Formula 1 motor-racing were more likely to be smokers as that company was sponsored by cigarette manufacturers.

Socio-cultural factors related to addictive behavior – smoking

Social learning theory (learning of behavior from the example of others) – shows that in studies in the US and the UK, 80% of children from non-smoking homes had never tried to smoke, and where parents smoked, half the children attempted smoking (Bauman, 1990). Peer-group pressure was shown to be more important amongst white Americans where the group norms were more important than parental influence, than amongst Hispanic and Asian-American where parental, rather than peer influence was dominant (Unger, 2001). Also a national study of US smoking in 2007 highlighted that smoking was more prevalent below the poverty line (over 30%) than above the poverty line (20%).

Examine prevention strategies and treatments for substance abuse and addictive behavior.

Promotion of anti-smoking campaigns by WHO (World Health Organization) – (cognitive/socio-cultural): they reckon that in two out of three countries worldwide, people are not even aware of the dangers of smoking. The WHO has been promoting a multi-point plan involving the encouragement of raising taxes on alcohol, enforcing the banning of advertizing cigarettes (including advertizing through their sponsorship of sporting events), using anti-smoking advertizing on cigarette packets and billboards, protecting people from secondary smoking in some public areas, and promoting services targeted at helping smokers to quit the habit.

Inducing competitive social pressure at school: for example, the study of Hanewinkel and Wiborg (2002) on primary prevention of smoking amongst children: "Be smart. Don't start". Carried out with over 2,000 12-13 year old students in Germany from over 100 classes, the test groups were to enter a competition, with special benefits for classes that would decide to be non-smoking for the six-month period of the study. The result showed that a third of those in the control group smoked, whilst only a quarter did in the test group. This experiment showed that this approach had some success as primary prevention (preventing people from smoking in the first place).

Treatments – following the work of Pisinger (2008) (also the study of Olsen et al in Denmark, 2006), the most effective combination of treatments is a combination of physiological (drug-based), and cognitive/socio-cultural (consultations with/support of cessations instructor, and groups such as smokers' anonymous). Physiologically, the most effective seems to have been Zyban – a nicotine-replacement therapy. This relieves the withdrawal symptoms (see earlier under biological factors relating to addictive behavior – be prepared to expand in an exam if necessary, especially on the issue of acetylcholine receptors, as above) and blocks the effect of nicotine if smoking is resumed. Psychologically, the strongest support came from a combination of counseling from a specialist in the field (cessation instructor – which turned out to be far more effective than with a nurse or doctor), combined with group support from anonymous groups.

Discuss factors related to overeating and the development of obesity.

WHO (World Health Organization) claims that there are **more than one billion adults** in the world who are overweight, with about of a third of them being clinically obese. WHO claims that overweight is now affecting more people than malnutrition and hunger, and is also widespread in developing, as well as developed countries. The ideal weight is below a **BMI** (body-mass index) of 25. This is calculated by taking the person's weight (in kg) and dividing it by the square of the height (in meters). A BMI of 25 plus is overweight, and over 30 is obese.

Obesity and overweight are generally a result of imbalance between stored fat and energy used for physical activity, respiration, and maintaining blood-pressure. Thus it is linked to lack of exercise, and consuming relatively more fat than carbohydrates.

Biological factor relating to overeating and development of obesity: genetic predisposition

The empirical study of Stunkard et al (1990) researched 93 pairs of twins who were reared apart, and compared their BMIs. They found that genetic factors accounted for about two-thirds of the variance in their body weight. The conclusion was that there were strong genetic factors in the development of obesity, and that genetics played an even greater role in those twins who were slim.

The genetic factor in obesity is not clear for the following reason. It is not clear to what degree the main factor is the role of genes in metabolism, or the role of genes in the number of fat cells. In addition, critics of the role of genes in obesity argue that the phenomenon of widespread obesity has occurred over too short a period for the genetic makeup of the population to have changed substantially.

Biological factor relating to overeating and development of obesity: evolution

It has been hypothesized, but not proven, that humans are genetically programmed to eat when food is available in order to store for times of shortage. This worked well during evolutionary (i.e. natural) selection, where Mankind was a species of hunter-gatherers, but is now biologically inappropriate, as food is abundant.

Cognitive factor related to overeating and obesity: unrealistic expectations from dieting

Many obese people start, break, and restart their diets – causing a yo-yo effect. When on a diet (especially one that goes to below hunger levels at 800 calories/day) with unrealistically high expectations, a person becomes extremely responsive to external cues (e.g. the smell of food, or feeling emotionally down) and can result in the 'what-the-hell' effect. It is where one little 'transgression', for example an ice-cream 'breaks' the diet, leading to an all-out binge of high calorie items, e.g. chocolate cookies, with feeling of utter failure, and restarting the diet only to end on the same cycle.

In other words, this cocktail of false hopes and unattainable criteria for success can explain lack of achievement in dieting and an overall weight gain rather than loss.

Socio-cultural factor related to obesity: sedentary lifestyle

The study of Prentice & Jebb (1995) studied changes in physical activity in a UK sample. The researchers acknowledged that there had been a significant decrease in food intake since 1970. The increase in obesity appeared correlated to aspects of the increasingly sedentary lifestyle: increase in car-ownership, and hours of television viewing. However, the data they used was correlational; thus unable to show an cause-and-effect relationship.

The Prentice & Jebb research was followed by a wider study conducted by the British *Foresight Report on Tackling Obesities* (2007), which concluded that obesity was an inevitable consequence of a society flooded with energy-dense cheap foods, labor-saving devices, motorized transport, and sedentary work.

Discuss prevention strategies and treatments for overeating and obesity.

Prevention strategy: Australia's 'go for your life' anti-obesity campaign (primary prevention – to avoid obesity in the first place) for children under-12, involving:

- Drinking tap-water rather than sweet drink.
- Increasing active play; decreasing 'screen-time' (computer games, videos, television).
- Include fruit and vegetables in the lunch-box.
- Limit 'sometimes' food items (chocolates, soft drinks, lolly-ices).
- Daily active physical exercise.
- Walking rather than riding to school and other activities where possible (Stride and ride)

Prevention and treatment strategy: dieting (secondary prevention – to avoid further obesity and also to reduce weight)

Blair-West (2007) set up a four-feature treatment program in Australia including:

*Realistic goal setting – loss of about 8% of body weight in one year.
*Low-sacrifice diet - eat less, but not completely sacrifice what is most fun to eat.
*Physical activity on a regular and systematic basis.
*Information on the dangers of being overweight and suitable dieting available to the public.

The above does not just involve cutting food intake, but seeks to combine it with a **habitual healthy lifestyle** including physical activity – in itself reducing the craving for inappropriate food substances in inappropriate amounts.

Prevention and treatment strategy: CBT (Cognitive Behavioral Therapy)

This aims to adjust cognition (what you think of diet-associated issues) to your objectives (losing, and then maintaining appropriate weight). The CBT program – based on the work of Beck (2005), involves three simultaneous programs:

1. Challenging eating behaviors – learning to recognize and adjust destructive eating patterns, monitoring calorie intake, seeking satisfying alternatives to social and emotionally-based eating, and keeping to a suitable exercise program.
2. Challenging cognitions – confront defeatist feelings that the weight will never come off, improve body image and self-confidence, increase social support.
3. Long-term maintenance of weight loss – e.g. strengthen motivation skills that can deal with challenging situations, and coping skills that avoid turning temporary setbacks into permanent ones.

According to Beck, the important thing is not the cause of over-eating, but dealing with the cognitions that lead to eating. CBT must focus on combating the permission-giving mechanism that leads to overeating – e.g. 'I am upset, therefore I may overeat'. [The participants in her program were 10 women who weighted between 90 and 136 kg. A year later, all women had lost weight and kept it off.]

SECTION THREE – HEALTH PROMOTION

Examine models and theories of health promotion *(for example, health belief model, stages of change model)*

Health promotion may be defined as the encouragement of people to change their lifestyle to reach their optimum level of health.

Psychology has a distinct role in health promotion. It is accepted that healthy living is in the interests of the public. It is also accepted that people in general will follow an appropriately healthy lifestyle if they perceive that they will physically suffer by not doing so – for examples smoking, excessive alcohol intake, not regularly exercising, or having too many sugary soft drinks.

Psychology therefore attempts to understand the cognitive barriers to living healthily, and ways to motivate the person to identify the barriers, deal with them, and attempt to overcome them. Some or all of these may be framed in the following models: **the health-belief model,** and the **stages of change model.**

The health-belief model (Rosenstock et. al. 1988) focuses on two simultaneous sets of forces that motivate the individual to address behavior adverse to health, such as smoking.

The first set of forces comes from the person – how you think. How far do you believe your life is in danger by smoking? Do you believe that you should give up smoking? Do you see benefits by not smoking? Do you believe you can give up smoking, given the benefits?

The second set of forces comes from the environment – the persuasive anti-smoking media campaign, including the government health warning on the cigarette packet.

These forces combine – and the more powerful they are, the more likely they are to promote a positive health change, such as serious determination to quit smoking. This has been shown by **the work of Quist-Paulsen and Gallefors (2003).** This experimental study focused on two groups of heart patients that were quitting smoking. The control group was given supportive group counseling. The members of the test group were given additional individualized phone support from the nursing staff. They aroused fear by warning about the serious heart-disease-related dangers of relapsing into smoking. The result was that 57% of the test group, but only 37% of the control group managed to quit. The rest could not avoid relapsing into smoking. The ethical issues of fear arousal in the test group were justified by the substantially higher rate of successful quitting at the end of the program, and the support offered by the nurses such as advising medication to stop the craving.

Strengths of the model

    (a) Identifies the issues and paradigm shifts faced in seeking a healthier lifestyle
    (b) Enables perceived barriers to be identified and addressed by psychologists.
    (c) Identifies the powerful environmental cues, such as those in West and Sohal (below).

Weaknesses of the model

    (a) Does not sufficiently factor-in the difficulties of applying the consistent will-power and persistence required to follow effectively a healthier lifestyle.
    (b) Those on lower incomes may not be able to afford the supportive environment of a fitness center or even the more expensive required healthier food.

The stages of change model focuses on a five stages of change that a person must go through to break a habit, e.g. smoking, excessive eating:

(a) Pre-contemplation – "I know I shouldn't smoke, but that's me."
(b) Contemplation – "I do need to quit, but I am not up to quitting."
(c) Preparation – "I'm taking the first steps to quit by not smoking until midday."
(d) Action – "I've stopped smoking."
(e) Maintenance – "I've stopped smoking over a long period and will never go back." This comes from consistent will-power and persistence.

A serious quitter will try to *progress* from stages (a) to (e). However, his will-power and persistence might keep him on track during the busy week at school/work, only to *relapse* into smoking during a lonely weekend. He might go back to stage (b) or even stage (a).

This model has been criticized by **the work of West and Sohal (2006).** This study compared the process of change involved in ex-smokers, and those who seriously attempted to quit but relapsed at least once. They found little evidence to support the spectrum of change from stages (a) to (e) above. Indeed, they found that it was the unplanned efforts to quit smoking (like the cue from the environment that it's "stop now or die soon", or the influence and support of friend who successfully quit) that were more effective than those attempts that followed the spectrum.

Strengths of the model

(a) Adaptable to wide variety of health-adverse behaviors including smoking, excessive alcohol intake, and overeating.
(b) Enables the stages of progress and associated barriers to be identified and addressed by psychologists.
(c) Does factor-in the difficulties of applying the consistent will-power and persistence required to follow a healthier lifestyle effectively.

Weaknesses of the model

(a) Does not sufficiently accommodate the social and cultural factors that might be involved in habit-changing decisions.
(b) Does not place sufficient weight on the powerful environmental cues, such as those in West and Sohal (above).

Discuss the effectiveness of health-promotion strategies

Reminder: health promotion may be defined as the encouragement of people to change their lifestyle to reach their optimum level of health.

Health promotion is conducted through the national campaigns with the mass media, through the workplace, and through the community at 'grass-roots' level.

Health promotion through the mass media – Australia's National Tobacco Strategy (NTS)

Conducted 2004-2009, the NTS used TV spots to use shock tactics to persuade smokers to quit, including videos of acute suffering from mouth cancer and lung cancer. The same pictures were reinforced by the NTS promoting their message by taking large newspaper advertisements, and pictures of smoking-induced tumors on cigarette packages.

The purpose of the campaign was to alert the public to the dangers of smoking, shock people into quitting, and support those who had already quit not to return to smoking.

The work of Beiner et al. (2006) during the Australia NTC focused on what single element had been the greatest help to some 800 smokers who had quit the previous two years. Over 30% said anti-smoking advertisements, with young quitters emphasizing the fear and sadness arising from the powerful and poignant ways the anti-smoking message was delivered. In contrast, only 21% cited conventional cessation units and nicotine-replacement therapy, and just 7% emphasized medication. Thus the mass-media's appropriately targeted and appropriately expressed anti-tobacco campaigns appear effective.

Health promotion through the workplace – many companies worldwide run such programs

The connection between health promotion and the workplace benefits both the company and the employees in terms of reducing the number of sick-leave absences, employee-borne health-insurance costs, and workers' compensation costs.

These programs tend to include health-promotion material on eating habits, smoking, and alcohol intakes, as well as on exercise and stress management. Typically, people from many different cultures meet at the workplace. Thus the workplace can reach many people from different cultural backgrounds. Through them, the health promotion messages spread through many cultures.

The work of Chapman (2005) combined studies of a large number of very different workplaces conducted in the previous 23 years. He found that health promotion campaigns produced a drop of more than a quarter in worker absenteeism, health costs, and workers' compensation costs. Thus the work place seems to be an effective area for health promotion, with very likely non-factored-in spreading the message to friends and families of those who benefited from the campaign.

Health promotion through the community – at 'grass-roots' level

The Florida-based TRUTH anti-tobacco campaign (1998-9) was aimed at changing teens' attitudes towards smoking, and encouraging them to form groups to influence yet more teens to do so. Central to this youth movement against smoking was its well-publicized confrontation with representatives of the tobacco industry, accusing them of manipulating the public to smoke. Its campaign to prevent and stop teenage smoking was wide ranging – including TV advertisements, billboards, the Internet, and local youth advocacy groups.

The communication efficacy of the campaign was measured after its first six months by a telephone survey. It showed that 92% of teens had heard of the campaign. And a survey of youth in the state conducted in 1999 showed that the number of smokers had gone down: by some 20% at middle schools, and 8% at high schools.

The work of Schum and Gold (2007) studied the TRUTH campaign. Aware of the above statistics (making it one of the most successful anti-smoking campaigns in the United States), it cited the following reasons for the campaign's success – which are vital points to note when planning future health-promotion initiatives and strategies:

   (a) It was conducted at grass roots level – being planned by teens for teens, it spoke to teens in ways that they could readily respond. Their passion for the campaign caught others - quickly.
   (b) It did much towards establishing a youth social norm: 'It's not cool to smoke'.

(c) It made use of teens' own social networks, which were out of reach of more conventional approaches. It was indeed the teens who delivered the message. This highlights the potential of Facebook health-promotion programs at grass-roots level.

POSSIBLE EXAMINATION QUESTIONS

LONG ANSWER QUESTIONS ONLY ON PAPER TWO

(a) Describe two stressors.
(b) Discuss strategies of coping with stressors.

Discuss prevention strategies and treatments for substance abuse and addictive behavior.

Evaluate any two health promotion strategies.

CHAPTER SEVEN – HUMAN RELATIONSHIPS

Paper 2 – option topic

Remember that you are applying the biological, cognitive, and socio-cultural perspectives to specific issues within the field of human relationships.

Orientation

Psychologists focus on studying human relationships in order to understand and enhance the ways in which people interact with one another.

The biological perspective emphasizes the work of neurotransmitters, hormones, and genes. Cognitive theorists apply schema theory, focusing on how we 'read' and interpret the behavior of others. Socio-cultural psychologists concentrate on social learning theory, attribution theory, social identity theory, and the influence of culture on the individual and the group. These three perspectives may be directed at issues such as those discussed in the main body of this chapter, including:

(a) **Stepping forward to help a person when in great need.** Biologists emphasize factors such as the degree of closeness (Madsen et al. 2007). Cognitivists would think of the need to avoid unpleasant feelings of arousal (as in Piliavin 1994). Socio-cultural psychologists might look at the degree of one's religious background (e.g. Colasanto, 1989). These individual approaches do not necessarily exclude one-another.

(b) **What attracts us to that 'special' individual.** Biologists consider what might stimulate the nervous and endocrine systems into the falling-in-love mode (e.g. Fisher, 2004). Cognitivists will be typically concerned with our recognizing loveable similarities in one another (e.g. Markey et. al 2007). Socio-culturalists might look at the degree of openness and acceptance when communicating (e.g. Collins and Miller, 1994).

(c) **How being bullied affects the victim.** Biologists typically view cortisol levels in the blood stream (Carney and Hazler 2007), cognitivists emphasize how the victim compares him/herself to someone else in a worse situation: 'many have suffered more than I have' (Thompson 2000), and socio-culturalists could look at the issue of those with aggressive anti-social behavior being likely to be bullied in the long run (Snyder, 2003), and its effects of promoting a vicious circle.

You, the student, should consider the question: 'To what extent do biological, cognitive and sociocultural factors influence human relationships?' in view of the theories and studies including those above.

As you progress with this topic, you should be evaluating the theories and studies relevant to the study of human relationships. You should be aware of methodological issues (such as in Piliavin 1994), the degree of artificiality of the study (e.g. Zimbardo, 1969), and the ethical issues including deception (as in Kieser and Baral, 1970).

SECTION ONE – SOCIAL RESPONSIBILTY AND ALTRUISM

Distinguish between altruism and pro-social behaviour.

Altruism is helping another person even when there is no observable benefit or reward in doing so. For example, when someone anonymously donates a sum of money to a worthy cause.

Pro-social behavior is when one's conduct helps another. For example, someone's car breaks down, and you offer to help. The purest forms of pro-social behavior are motivated by altruism, an unselfish interest in helping another person. The circumstances most likely to evoke altruism are empathy for an individual in need, or a close relationship between the benefactor and the recipient.

Many pro-social behaviors that appear altruistic are in fact motivated by the norm of reciprocity, which is the obligation to return a favor with a favor. People feel guilty when they do not reciprocate and they may feel angry when someone else does not reciprocate.

Example of pro-social behavior - that which was investigated in Piliavin et al's research (1969, see below), which illustrates coming forward to help possibly to avoid unpleasant feelings and possible benefits of recognition. That would be pro-social, but not necessarily altruistic.

Piliavin et als' experimental research involved set-up 'crises' at various locations on the New York subway, between 11am and 3pm. The 'victims' were young men aged 25-35. One involved a drunken man, smelling of alcohol, with another bottle of drink in his bag. The other involved a sober victim with his cane. A set-up 'model helper' was instructed to come forward if no help was offered within 70 seconds. There were covert observers recording the findings.

The observers noted both qualitative and quantitative data – speed of help, gender of helper, frequency of help, verbal comments, and degree of tendency to move away from the victim. Thus non-participant covert observation was the means of obtaining data for this experimental research.

Results - in the 103 trials, 93% of the time someone helped spontaneously, and 60% of the time, more than one helper was involved. The cane victim got help all the time, the drunk just over 80% of the time. There was no diffusion of responsibility observed (see under bystanderism, below), even with increase in group size.

Piliavin argues that the theory emerging from the responses to the crises may be based on a very quick cost-reward analysis, involving weighing up the cost of helping (e.g. chance of physical harm) against cost of not helping (e.g. feelings of guilt). Also taken into account are the rewards of helping (e.g. approval of those watching) against the rewards of not helping (e.g. time saved).

Thus the findings on the New York subway experiment may be explained by the arousal-cost-reward model, such as someone stepping out to help in each scenario with the cane-carrying person (cost of help is low and cost of not helping is high), and the fewer people stepping forward to help the drunk based on the commonly-perceived revulsion towards drunken behavior, and in the notion that he should never have been drunk in the first place.

Evaluation: the experiment which was carried out in the field had ecological validity, obtaining a lot of detailed data. The procedures that were repeated were standardized. However, there were methodological weaknesses. Fewer of the trials took place with the drunk than with the cane. And though the procedures were well-standardized, it was not clear how many of the observation-based findings (DVs), such as moving towards or away from the victim, were recorded accurately.

Ethically, this research also needed to account for the involved deception, lack of consent, lack of debriefing, and the causing of anxiety to members of the public.

Contrast two theories explaining altruism in humans.

(a) Explanation of altruism: evolutionary.

Kin-selection theory (as exemplified in Dawkins: 'The Selfish Gene') theorizes that we have an innate drive for the preservation of our species as a whole, and this drive becomes more acute as those suffering are closer to ourselves. ('Closer' meaning immediate relatives and friends – the closer you feel to the person, the more you feel their pain.) **Kin-selection theory suggests that we should favor close family members when times are hard.** Applies to humans and animals alike – since those many groups share many genes, altruistic behavior promotes the preservation of the many genes identical to our own, and ensures that they are passed to the next generation. Evaluation – this is supported by the tendency to go to extreme lengths to protect those closest to us (family, friends).

In addition, studies with animals suggest the biological base for kin-selection. Vampire bats are more likely to share blood with 'roost-mates', and it appears that they have sufficient cognition to guarantee recognition of cooperators and defectors (Wilkinson, 1984). Squirrels are more likely to warn relatives than non-relatives for predators (Sherman, 1980).

With people, the work of Madsen et al. (2007) indicate that humans are more likely to help relatives (kin selection) in emergency situations than complete strangers. This study used male and female students in two locations: the UK and South Africa.

All participants supplied the researchers with a list of blood relatives of various degrees of closeness. One relative (close or distant) was selected randomly by the researchers. Then each participant had to sit in an uncomfortable position – thighs parallel to the ground, back to the wall. They were paid for every 20-seconds that they sat in that painful way. The money would not be given to them, but to the selected relative. Results – the closer the relative, the longer the endurance of the painful position, and this was even more distinct in male participants than in female participants. The degree of closeness was slightly less marked amongst the Zulus of South Africa, who tended to equate siblings and cousins in their desire to support them.

Evaluation – it does appear that kin-selection is a strong motivator for altruistic behavior. In addition, two cultures were selected on the grounds of their having different social concepts of the meaning of 'kin' and 'family'. Therefore the biological evolutionary argument would be strengthened if the biological degree of closeness would determine readiness to help in two very difficult cultures. It may be criticized on the grounds that the gifts to family members were relatively trivial in terms of the needs of the family-member recipients (though in the UK, the initial 40 pence per 20 seconds was raised during the course of the study), and some participants might have had sufficiently high pain thresholds to take the sitting position in their stride.

The empathy-altruism model (Toi and Batson, 1982) suggests that a human being has evolved to feel two types of distress in the suffering of a fellow-human: **personal distress, and empathic concern** – which illustrates Batson's famous experimental study involved female psychology students listening to audio-tapes centered on a student named Carol. She talked about the accident, the injuries she sustained, and her anxiety on not being able to complete the program. The objectives – would they help Carol by writing to her, or meet up with her and sharing their lecture notes? One group of students had the tapes presented with a high level of empathy – where the experimenter framed the experiences within getting the students to focus on how Carol was feeling. The second group was told not to be concerned with her feelings – a low level of empathy. The researchers also divided the participants into two groups: high cost for not helping, and low cost for not helping. The high-cost group was told that Carol would see them again in class, and the low cost group were informed that she would complete her studies out of class. The results were that those in the high empathy group were as likely as not to help Carol whether they believed they would see Carol again in class, whereas those in the low-empathy group were more prepared to help where they were informed that Carol would return to class.

However, this experiment did not look at the personalities and backgournds of those involved. Indeed, it is not clear whether empathy is something learnt (socio-cultural) or something biologically based.

(b) Explanation of altruism: dispositional factors versus situational factors.

You show altruism because you are brought up to show concern for others, or your religious belief requires you to do so. Your motives are dispositional.

You show altruism because you happen to have arrived an hour early at that place and have nothing else to do. Your motives are situational.

Socio-cultural: religious training – the 'Good Samaritan' study (Darley & Bateson, 1973) tested whether it was religious devotion that increased the likelihood of offering help **(dispositional factor),** or whether it was the convenience of the moment that increased the likelihood **(situational factor).** The sessions were held at the Princeton Theological Seminary. In the first session, the students in the study were given a questionnaire measuring the degree of the personal religiosity of the student. In the second, the students were divided into two. One group was told that they would be giving a presentation on suitable career openings for seminary graduates, and the second group was required to give a detailed exposition on the parable of the Good Samaritan. These presentations would take place in a building some distance elsewhere on campus. At the end of the instruction, they were put into three groups prior to the instruction - (mixed as regards to the subject of the presentation) – 'you must hurry to get over at once to deliver' 'you should get over as soon as possible' and 'you may go over now' – (high pressure, medium pressure, and low pressure). On the way, there was a set –up – a person who had passed out in an alleyway. Results – only 10% helped when under high pressure to hurry, 45% under moderate pressure, and 63% in the low pressure to hurry situation. Conclusions – willingness to help appears to have been situational (degree of pressure to hurry) rather than dispositional (religious training, impact of the subject of their planned presentations).

Evaluation: the experiment was set up in a community where the religious commitment to help others was present, and its significance was taken into account within the study. The experimental nature of the study was strengthened in the second stage by mixing those who prepared the 'control' (career) presentation and those who prepared the 'test' (the Good Samaritan). However, the experiment was limited in scope in that it only investigated the conflict situation – when a situational factor goes against the dispositional factor. Indeed, the study of **Colasanto (1989)** indicated that both students and members of the general public that were religiously committed were more likely to give time and money to those in need where situational factors were not conflicting issues.

Ethically, this research also needed to account for the involved deception.

Using one or more research studies, explain cross-cultural differences in prosocial behaviour.

The extensive studies of Levine et al (1994) assessed the helpfulness of strangers in 36 cities in the US and 23 cities elsewhere in the world. The experiments involved every-day assistance: a passing pedestrian returning a dropped pen, a man with an injured leg getting help whilst struggling to retrieve a fallen magazine, and a blind person struggling to negotiate a busy intersection.

Within the US, the most helpful cities were those in the south, whilst the much larger ones in the north east and California were least helpful – thus likelihood of being helped seemed to drop as city population increased. **In the blind person experiment in international cities,** help was offered every time in Rio (Brazil), San Jose (Costa Rica), Lilongwe (Malawi), Madrid (Spain), and Prague (Czech Republic). Help was offered less than half the time in Kuala Lumpur (Malaysia) and Bangkok (Thailand).

However, the expectation that 'slower-paced' cities would be more helpful than the 'faster-paced' did not always hold good: fast-paced, first-world cities of Copenhagen and Vienna were very kind to strangers, whilst their counterparts in slower-paced Kuala Lumpur were not helpful at all. It was also noted that the general personality of the city affected non-native residents: both Brazilians and Thais were more likely to offer help in Rio than in Manhattan, New York.

The explanations given were:

(a) The norms of the society – as to whether it was appropriate to seek help from others or not.

(b) The presence or absence of a culture of helping strangers. For example the Spanish and Latin American-based notion of 'simpatico' – proactive concern with the well-being of others that even extends to strangers in difficulty.

(c) The economic status of the city was less significant. Some cities with much poverty (e.g. Rio, Lilongwe, San Jose, and Calcutta) had a culture of helping strangers, as did others that were comparatively wealthy (e.g. Copenhagen, Madrid, Vienna). Others did not appear to have that culture (wealthy or poor), and gave relatively little help (e.g. New York, Singapore, Kuala Lumpar, Bagkok

(d) The degree of perceived anonymity in the city: typically (but not always) the larger the city, the less people feel connected to each other.

The Levine studies had high ecological validity. They were simple everyday situations which were easily replicable in cities worldwide. However, they may be criticized on the grounds of:

(a) The correctness of interpreting the three above tasks as evidence of pro-social behavior.

(b) Some local circumstances discouraging helping behavior – e.g. in New York people might be suspicious that the exercise is a publicity scam and might be verbally abusive.

Examine factors influencing bystanderism.

In 1964, Kitty Genovese was stabbed to death by a serial murderer and rapist, over a half-hour period. Though witnessed by 38 of her neighbors, not one of them even telephoned for help. This type of behavior is termed bystanderism. Research by Latané and Darley suggests that bystanderism occurs for two reasons: diffusion of responsibility and pluralistic ignorance.

Diffusion of Responsibility – the more people around, less the individual is likely to come forward, relying on others to do so. **This was tested by Latané and Darley (1968),** whereby participants were interviewed over the intercom on the topic of living in a high-pressure urban environment. Some students were told that they were being interviewed on their own, others were told that there would be a smaller number of co-interviewees, and further participants were told that it would be a large number. In fact, all the other voices were simulated on the intercom system. While the research was in progress, there were a series of loud choking noises – the sounds of an immediate emergency. Results: those believing themselves to be the only ones there helped 85% of the time, when they thought that there were a few others there, 65%, but when it went up to the belief that there were four others, the number went down to 31%.

Pluralistic Ignorance – people look around at others to see their reactions as cues in how to act in an emergency situation. **Tested by Latané and Darley (1969),** a set of emergency screams associated with a call and a female cry were set up next door to a waiting room. When a single individual was alone in that waiting room, he or she would be more likely to help. However, there was less altruistic behavior when there were many in the waiting room. Thus the presence of others in the room tended to reinforce the inherent ambiguity in the situation.

These studies were ecologically valid as they were set up in environments where these situations might well actually have occurred. There were no difficulties in the simply observing whether help would be offered or not. They may be criticized for the small number of participants – there were only 40 in the 1969 study. They also ignored the differences in competence and experience of those deciding whether to come forward to help or not. There could have been issues with, for example, the mood of the people of the time.

See also Piliavin's study of bystanderism/willingness to offer help on the New York subway, above.

SECTION TWO – INTERPERSONAL RELATIONSHIPS

Examine biological, psychological, and social origins of attraction.

The biological basis of attraction and love: all animals, including humans, display much of the same behavior when attracted to the opposite sex. Males will compete to get the highest quality females for passing on their genes. The females usually (but not with all species in the animal kingdom) take care of the young alone. In humans, females look for the male who can provide well and make her feel secure.

Romantic love is not an emotion, but a **hormone-based motivation system.** It creates a deep craving to cause lovers to mate and reproduce. Romantic love is characterized by obsession towards the sweetheart, making the head spin and the heart throb. This is created by a romantic biological cocktail. It is composed of adrenaline (makes your palms sweat and mouth go dry in the presence of that special someone), adjustment of serotonin levels (which speeds up the nervous system), secretion of oxytocin (a powerful hormone released by both men and women during touching and in sex – which deepens and intensifies feelings of attachment), and vasopressin (released during sex, which promotes long-term commitment).

The work of Wedekind (1995) suggests that **MHC (major histo-compatibility complex) - genetic compatibility** guides us in partner preferences. MHC genes are co-dominant, meaning that both sets of inherited genes have an effect on the child's immune system. That means that the more diverse the MHC genes of the parents, the stronger the immune systems of the children. Both sexes have evolved to ensure their own survival by applying their genes to the creation of the healthiest possible children. With his 'dirty shirt' experiment, he demonstrated that women preferred the scent of men with dissimilar genes, though those on oral contraceptives preferred those with similar genes.

The dirty shirt experiment involved 49 women and 44 men with a wide range of MSC genes... the men had to avoid aftershave with odor and eat non-spicy food for two days, and wear the new t-shirt supplied for two nights in row. The women had to smell the t-shirts after they were returned – used, but unwashed. Three of the boxes of t-shirts were from MHC-dissimilar, three were from MHC-similar t-shirts, and one contained an unworn t-shirt as a control. The women were asked to rate the odors of each of the t-shirts as pleasant or unpleasant. Overall, the results showed that women preferred the scent of men with dissimilar genes, though those on oral contraceptives preferred those with similar genes.

Cognitive perspectives in attraction and love

(a) Morry (2007) **'attraction-similar' model**, proposes that people select both friends and partners on the bases of their being perceived as similar to themselves...

This model was researched by Markey et al (2007), which assessed the extent that similarity was a factor as a basis of choosing partners. They used questionnaires where participants supplied information on (i) the characteristics and attitudes of their ideal romantic partner without thinking of anyone in particular (ii) their own characteristics and attitudes; and in a follow-up (iii) similar questions to couples who had been together for more than a year. The studies confirmed that people want partners similar to themselves. The study is supported for the relatively large sample (including 106 couples), but may be criticized because perception and actual behavior may not always be congruent (the same, in line with each other).

It may also be criticized because in reality it may not be just that **similarity promotes attraction,** but that **attraction promotes similarity**. The study of Davis and Rusbult (2001) demonstrated that attraction can also foster similarity – as one idealizes the partner's behavior, he/she adjusts to its flow. Indeed, the above research of Markey et al (2007) raised the issue of *reciprocity*: people often view their own partners more positively than they view themselves. And in idealizing their behavior, they tend to find themselves influenced by them.

(b) Kieser and Baral (1970) evaluated the **importance of self-esteem in relationship formation.** Those who feel great about themselves are going to be far more proactive and successful in attracting a quality partner. They investigated their hypothesis by giving a fake IQ test to a group of men. The scores they gave them were entirely untrue. One group (individual by individual, in privacy) was told that they scored 'off the charts' – the highest scores ever seen on the IQ test. The second group was told (individual by individual, in privacy) that there must have been something wrong, because their scores were so low – and that they should arrange to redo the test in the near future. After the scores were given, the individual men sat in the waiting room to be paid for taking part in the study. During that time, a very attractive female walked into the room. The experimenters found that the men who had received the self-esteem boost of high scores readily engaged in conversation with her, in contrast with the 'low scorers' who tended not to.

Social perspectives in attraction and love include a wide range of elements, for example:

- (a) Familiarity is more attractive than the unfamiliar (Zajonc et al, 1971): more exposure to the other increases the sense of trust. This was supported by the work of

Jorgensen and Cervone (1978), who found that people rated the photographs of strangers more highly the more often they saw them.

(b) Proximity: those spending time with us who live, study, and work near to us are more likely to be partners and friends material (Festinger 1950, based on his study of friendship patterns amongst university students).

(c) Social comparison: a person appears more attractive to those who have been less exposed to the extremely good looking than to those who have. This is illustrated by the experimental work of Kenrick & Gutierres (1980). The control group was asked to rate the attractiveness of an average looking woman. The test group was given the same task after watching *Charlie's Angels*, a television program starring three very attractive women. Those seeing the program rated the average woman as less attractive.

(d) People who make us feel good in their presence (Lewicky, 1985), and also those who we initially dislike and then change our minds (Aronson & Linder, 1965).

Discuss the role of communication in maintaining relationships.

(a) The work of Canary & Stafford (1994) identified five communicative strategies that keep a relationship alive:

(i) Spontaneity – doing things to make your partner feel good (unpredictability keeps a fun edge to the relationship).

(ii) Self-disclosure – sharing intimate things about oneself (see Collins and Miller, below).

(iii) Assurance and empathy – make the partner feel that his/her feelings are respected.

(iv) Social networking together – doing things together with friends and family.

(v) Sharing tasks together (the dishes: he washes, she dries).

(b) Interpretation of one's partner's communication is a function of the **current character of the relationship.** Where relationships are positive, attributions (good things) are biased towards the partner, and faults are seen as situational (not taken personally – see Chapter 3 on socio-cultural psychology). Unhealthy relationships are the opposite: 'You always...' and 'You never...' Bradbury and Fincham (1992) found that where wives communicated blame to the husband (made dispositional judgments) in negative situations, they were also more likely to behave negatively towards the husband in general.

(c) Those with a higher degree of self-disclosure (sharing facts of one's life, inner thoughts, and feelings) tend to foster trust – a key part of attachment. Collins and Miller (1994) found that people who share personal information are more liked than those who are more secretive. They also found that people disclose more intimate information to those they like. And the communication of being liked is in itself a positive force in maintaining a relationship.

Explain the role that culture plays in the formation and maintenance of relationships.

The socio-cultural perspective highlights that **forming and keeping a relationship is a function of cultural norms and expectations.** Levine et al (1995) found that participants in the countries that had a high standard of living and were individualist in outlook (putting needs of the individual before those of the community – e.g. the US) would rate love as vital to the decision to marry, and absence of it as sufficient reason to divorce. They found that divorce rates are highly correlated with the belief that the disappearance of love is enough cause to end the marriage. Goodwin (1995) argues that passionate love as we know it is largely a western phenomenon: the attitude from non-western societies with the norm of the arranged marriage is that **westerners marry those they love, whilst they love those they marry**. The study of Gupta and Singh (1992) found that couples in India who married for love reported lower levels of love after five years than those whose marriages had been arranged. Indeed, Dion and Dion (1993) highlight that in traditional societies marriage is seen as an alliance between two families (rather than two individuals): for having children, and also economic and social support.

The work of Yelsma & Athappilly (1988) studied marriage satisfaction and communication practices of 28 Indian couples in arranged marriages, 25 Indian couples in 'love' marriages (marriages of choice), and 31 American couples. They found that those in arranged marriages had higher marital relationship satisfaction scores than either the love-married people in India or the sample in the United States. Thus romance and passion would appear to have little long-term impact. However the study may be criticized on its reliance on questionnaire surveys, and the very different expectations of those in arranged marriages, and those in marriages of their own choice.

Analyse why relationships may change or end.

The work of Levinger (1980) indicates that relationships will end when:

(i) Problems seem insoluble, with a divorce/break-up as the only means of escape to a new life. (This could include situational issues such as completely different working hours, and prolonged pressure of work.)

(ii) Little faith that the marriage will endure, and lack of commitment to make it succeed.

(iii) Other more 'desirable' partners are readily available.

The work of Canary & Dainton (2003) goes even further when suggesting that relationships by nature have a natural tendency to end. Problems tend to accelerate the process of leaving a relationship and changing partners:

In addition, studies show that the breakdown of relationships will occur where there are:

(a) Negative patterns of accommodation – the process of responding to a partner's negative behavior can cause the nature of the relationship to be changed (Rusbult et al. 1991). Positive accommodation includes discussing problems openly, waiting for the situation to improve naturally, and forgiving each other. Negative accommodation includes physical avoidance, silent treatment, and recounting previous failures.

(b) Relationship without equity, which tends to suffer more than relationship with equity. The equity theory of love predicts that people are happiest where benefits and costs are balanced, so that both partners contribute and receive more or less the same. In a study of 2,000 couples, Hatfield (1979) found that those who felt they were not getting a fair, equitable deal in the relationship were the most likely to cheat on the relationship..

(c) Fatal attraction (Felmlee, 1995) – where the same trait that attracted leads to the breakup of the relationship – e.g. the 'good-girl / bad-boy' – the excitement of being with a 'bad-boy' with motor-biking adventures gives way to the unpleasantness of dealing with his irresponsibility and abuse. Also, a partner who travels a lot may bring the initial attraction of fascinating conversation, but the relationship may dissolve when facing the reality of the other never being at home.

In spite of best intentions, relationships do not always survive the many changes they experience over time. Duck (1992), using a series of longitudinal studies, identified the following factors which would work towards the dissolution of a marriage/relationship. These include: parents of one or both of the couple having divorced, teenage marriage, wide difference in educational and socio-economic background, many previous partners, and those in lower socio-economic groups.

SECTION THREE – VIOLENCE

Aggression – is where the goal is to dominate or harm another individual.

Violence is an aggressive act in abusing individuals - physically, verbally, or psychologically.

War and **genocide** are institutionalized and systematized forms of violence between groups.

Violent behavior may be divided into low-base and high-base behavior. **Low base violence** is difficult to observe and subtle, or takes place in isolated incidences over a long period of time, with an un-noticeable build-up.

Bullying – is where a person is *repeatedly* exposed to intentional negative actions on the part of one or more other people, which may be physical, verbal, or psychological. *Make sure that you can carefully link bullying to violence.*

Evaluate socio-cultural explanations of the origins of violence

(a) Power differences between different social groups (Vygotsky, 1930s) – traditionally, differences between groups are based on gender, social class, ethnicity, or religion. The more powerful group inflicts violence on the weaker group – physically, verbally, and/or psychologically. More powerful / less powerful groups include Nazis/Jews, Tutsi/Hutus, men/women, and parents/children. The violence comes with the at least tacit agreement of the population of the dominant group. This incorporates violent behavior within the social norm of the dominant group - towards specific weaker groups. For example, children will be spanked if social norms dictate that parents may spank their children. It could be argued that group violent behaviors are group survival mechanisms which are learned through social learning (modeling, see Chapter 3). Difficulties with the power-difference theory are (a) establishing cause and effect, and (b) drawing the line between violent behavior and e.g. the typical 'fun' horseplay between teenage boys.

(b) Deindividuation theory: a person appears to be less accountable for otherwise unacceptable or even violent behavior when the victim is part of a crowd, faceless, and anonymous. Soccer violence between the supporters of opposing teams is enabled by the other side dressing in colors which make them 'the faceless other'.

The classic study of deindividuation was carried out by Zimbardo (1969) involving participating female university students inflicting electric shocks under orders. Half of them were dressed in uniform lab coats and hoods that hid their faces, and were never referred to by name. The other half wore normal clothes and was personally identified by name tags. Both sets of participants could see the student being shocked. Participant "learning promoters" were given information on the students: either "she is honest, sincere, and warm" or "she is conceited and critical".

The faceless participant facilitators delivered twice as many shocks, and the amount of shock did not vary according to the description of the learner. Name-tagged participants varied the amount of shock according to the description given.

'Faceless others' were more likely to punish more severely for the wrong answers. Deindividuation had lowered their sense of caution and accountability. This model of deindividuation may explain mob violence, riots, military massacres, and police brutality.

Evaluation: the deindividuation lacked ecological validity. The perpetrators were completely anonymous in being uniformed and faceless, though it may help to explain the application of torture in interrogation in issues of national security. There is also the ethical concern that the participants may have been subjected to undue stress which long-term negative consequences.

The work of **Diener et al (1976),** carried out a naturalistic and experimental observation of children in the Halloween 'trick or treat' scenario. The aim was to observe whether deindividuation would cause children to take liberties. The children were divided into two groups. In the first one they gave their names and addresses (individuation, the control), and in the other one they remained anonymous (deindividualtion, the test, the independent variable being lack of individuation). The children were told to take one candy only. Those in the control took only one in 80% of the cases. Those in the test whose identities were not traceable complied by taking not more than one in only 8% of the cases. Conclusion – deindividuation reduces caution and takes away the need to be on best behavior.

Unlike Zimbardo carried out in laboratory conditions, this study had the advantage of ecological validity.

Discuss the relative effectiveness of two strategies for reducing violence

1. Anger management and empathy development: involving cognitive, counseling-based programs in schools, often involving altering people's immediate perceptions of cues which may promote unnecessary aggressive reactions. They include teaching participants to 'read' a situation. Dodge (1981) found that some children have a problem 'processing' social cues. Often well-meaning, but clumsy attempts to reach out in friendship can be read as having hostile intent, particularly if the people concerned have different senses of humor. Whilst immediate reactions are hostile, their more considered reactions are not. Once they have had a chance to think about it, they react in a more reasonable way. Teaching students to count to ten before reacting is one strategy. So is assertiveness training in anger management – getting the person who feels hostility to calmly ask the other what he/she 'meant by that'.

The work of Feshbach and Feschbach (1982) was focused on empathy training. It focused on educating elementary school children to imagine how they would feel if they were in the place of the bullied child. Playground observations of the test group given empathy showed a substantially lower rate of bullying that those in the control group who had not been given empathy. Indeed, Figueieredo et al (from 2007) are testing the long-term effects of a computer simulation in which the player works as friend and counselor to a bullied child in various scenarios. The overall goal is to encourage students to develop empathy, and social skills to face bullying, cope with bullying, and ultimately to help to create a non-bullying environment.

(b) Strategies for dealing with bullying (violent behavior) – peer counseling and mediation: – a select group of students is briefed in the skills of dealing with conflicts, including those involving bullying.

This peer counseling typically takes the form of both parties -- bully and victim -- coming together to discuss the problem *and* they both sign an agreement that details what each will do in the future if the problem arises again. Also, the mediators inform the students that a copy goes to the peer mediation coordinator and the assistant principal (or whoever is in charge of discipline). If a child breaks the agreement -- if the bully retaliates – s/he will be disciplined appropriately. It is important that mediation takes place before the boiling point is reached and physical assault occurs. If a bully continues in spite of mediation and/or discipline, the matter is taken to the next disciplinary level.

A school-based mediation program in Stow, Ohio (population 32,000), began in the high school in 1994. Counselors train students and staff in mediation techniques and effective communication, anger management, and conflict resolution skills. A core of over 25 student mediators works with staff to address problems referred by teachers, students, and disputants. The conflicts include disagreements over hallway confrontations, dating relationships, fights, and intimidation. In 1998, the school resource officer helped the student mediators and faculty members to confront and resolve over 100 disputes. The program continues to be well received by students, administrators, parent groups, and teachers.

Part of the program's success was based on the high level of organization: peer counseling appears to have been most effective where the program is responsibly coordinated and effectively supported by the school.

The effects of short-term and long-term exposure to violence

Reminder! Bullying is where a person is repeatedly exposed to negative actions of others, which may be physical, verbal, or psychological. *Make sure that you can carefully link bullying to violence.*

Effects of short and long term bullying on the individual – exemplified by the questionnaire-based study of **Elliot and Kirkpatrick (1999)** in the UK found a much higher attempted suicide rate in those who had been bullied (20%) than those who had not (3%). Several thousand students participated in the survey.

The work of Olweus (1992) (based on self-reported narrative and analysis) highlighted the short and long-term effects of bulling. In the short term, there is likely to be a fall in academic performance, more days off school for sickness, depression and even consideration of suicide. Long term effects, include difficulties in trusting people, low self-esteem, and tendency to opt out of society.

It is difficult to measure the net effect of bullying on the victims because of lack of data on the victimized students before the bullying began. As most of the data was based on self-report, it relied on the victim's attribution of cause and effect, often long after the bullying had stopped.

The role of cortisol (anti-stress hormones secreted by the adrenal glands) **on bullying levels in humans has been supported by the research of Carney and Hazler (2007).** The researchers measured cortisol levels in the saliva of 94 6th grade students between ages 9 and 14, and asked them to fill out a questionnaire on their experiences associated with bullying. Cortisol levels were measured (through saliva) first thing in the morning, and just before lunchtime - the time of the day when bullied students felt most threatened as there was a minimum of supervision.

There was a brief rise in cortisol levels - in the short term only. Those suffering long-term bullying seem to have lower cortisol levels – hypocortisol – linked to chronic fatigue, chronic pain, and PTSD (post-traumatic stress disorder). All types of bullying – physical, psychological, and verbal – seemed to be equally powerful in causing PTSD.

However the extent of the negative impact bullying has on its victims is modified and lessened by the perceptive and adaptive strategies employed by the victim, which include:

- Support of family and peers with whom victim may confide.

- The downward-comparison perspective – where the victim compares him/herself to someone else in a worse situation: 'many have suffered more than I have'.

- Having the power to positively influence and/or escape the bully, rather than feeling trapped (Kliewer et al, 2004).

But the likelihood of bullying increased where:

- The bullied was one of a group out of favor with the others. The Human Rights Watch Report (*Hatred in the Hallways* 2001) highlighted its strong probability with homosexual and lesbian students. 45% of males and 26% of females with those leanings suffered verbal and physical bullying.

- Those showing aggressive anti-social behavior were likely to be bullied in the long run (Snyder, 2003 – based in the UK – on a longitudinal study of 266 students from kindergarten to elementary school).

POSSIBLE EXAMINATION QUESTIONS

LONG ANSWER QUESTIONS ONLY ON PAPER TWO

Using one or more research studies, explain cross-cultural differences in pro-social behaviour.

Analyze why relationships may change or end.

Discuss the relative effectiveness of two strategies for reducing violence.

CHAPTER EIGHT – SPORT PSYCHOLOGY

Paper 2 – option topic

Remember that you are applying the biological, cognitive, and socio-cultural perspectives to specific issues within the field of sport psychology.

These issues are motivation in sport (how keen you are to participate individually or as a member of a team), skill development and performance (how you improve both as an individual athlete, and as a member of a team), and problems in sport (for example stress, burnout).

Sport psychology recognizes the contribution of sport to good health, and also to international and cross-cultural understanding – sports emphasizing the competitive and yet common ground. Sport psychology also addresses the roadblocks to progress in sport faced by individuals and teams.

Learning outcomes of this unit: General framework (applicable to all topics in the option)

To what extent do biological, cognitive and socio-cultural factors influence behavior in sports?

For biological influences, look at the following areas below:

- Arousal theories: The individual zone of optimal functioning theory (Hanin, 1997) – containing both biological and cognitive elements.
- The effects of drug use in sport.

For cognitive influences, look at the following areas below:

- Arousal theories: The individual zone of optimal functioning theory (Hanin, 1997) – as above.
- Goal setting: cognitive evaluative theory, self-efficacy theory,
- Motivation of individuals: Nicholl's achievement goal theory of motivation.
- Coping with sports injuries: the grief-reaction-response model (Harris, 2003), and the cognitive appraisal model (Udry et al, 1997).
- Coping with burnout: the cognitive-affective model (Smith, 1986), and the investment/entrapment model (Raedeke, 1997).

For socio-cultural influences, look at the following areas below:

- Motivation of individuals: how far coaches affect individual or team behavior in sport.
- The relationships between team cohesion and performance

Evaluate psychological research (that is, theories and/or studies) relevant to sport psychology.

For emotion and motivation, look at the following:

- Cognitive evaluation theory (Deci, 1975), and the work Ryan (1977).
- Self-efficacy theory (Bandura, 1977), and the work of Hochstetler et al. (1985).
- Nicholls' achievement goal theory of motivation (1984), and the work of Filby et al. (1999), Schofield et al. (2005)

For skill development and performance, look at the following

- Techniques for skill development used in sport: massed practice versus distributive practice, and the work of Singer (1965), Lee and Genovese (1988)
- Techniques for skill development used in sport: mental imagery, and the work of Martin et al. (1999), Callow and Hardy (2001).
- The relationship between team cohesion and performance, and the work of Carron (1982), and Patterson (2005).

For problems in sport, look at the following:

- Coming to terms with chronic sports injury: the grief-reaction-response model (Harris, 2003), the cognitive appraisal model (Udry et al. 1997).
- Identifying and coping with burnout: the cognitive-affective model (Smith, 1986), and the investment/entrapment model (Raedeke, 1997).

SECTION ONE – EMOTION AND MOTIVATION

Evaluate theories of motivation in sport (for example, cognitive-evaluation theory, self-efficacy theory).

If you are intrinsically motivated, you feel that you yourself want to do it and can do it (complete a marathon, learn to ski)!

If you are extrinsically motivated, you are pushed by external rewards (your coach's praise, the prospect of winning the $25,000 in prize money).

Cognitive evaluation theory (Deci, 1975) holds that your level of motivation in sport depends on two things working together:

(a) **Feeling of competence** – how far are you made to feel good about your sporting performance, such as receiving awards and positive encouragement from your coach?

(b) **Self-determination** – are you striving to get into you school's First XI soccer team because that is what you want, or that is what your father wants?

If the response to the first question is negative, you are less likely to improve because you are suffering negative **information.** You feel less competent. If the response to the second question is "I'm doing this only to make my family happy", you are also less likely to improve because you feel that you are not the decision-maker; you feel **controlled**.

For optimum motivation, there has to be combination of positive **intrinsic motivation** (e.g. you love karate and strive to improve) and **extrinsic motivation** (e.g. you want to be awarded the black belt in karate).

The work of Ryan (1977) investigated the effect of receiving an athletic scholarship on college-level football players' motivation. The study showed that those on scholarships felt less excited about the game (less intrinsic motivation), and enjoyed playing it less. This suggests that scholarships might work against the interests of the players optimizing their performances. However, the later study of Amorose & Horn (2000) indicated that the real reason for the scholarship holders' poorer motivation was the negative extrinsic reality of their coaches' expectations. For example, failure to score sufficient goals would mean the threat of losing the scholarship. Thus coaches who motivate with more positive feedback without negatively stressing the financial aspect of the situation would be most likely to motivate their athletes to maximize performance on the field.

Strengths of cognitive evaluation theory

1. Several follow-up studies have shown that both scholarships and negative perceptions of coaches have undermined athletes' performances.

2. The self-reporting research highlighted the sports scholars' ambivalent feelings towards the high expectations that they faced, and also towards their encounters with scholarship-barbed negative feedback.

Limitations of cognitive evaluation theory

1. Difficult to establish the precise causes of the levels of performance reached. The experiments were not laboratory-controlled.

2. The researchers relied on self-reports by the athletes to a great extent.

3. There are ethical issues in experimental research that offers the test group athletic scholarships, as the above studies suggest their association with deteriorating progress in sport.

Self-efficacy theory (Bandura, 1977) holds that your level of motivation in sport depends on your belief in how well you can perform. For example a person will happily sign up for a 10-kilometer run following a successful recent 10k on the fitness-room treadmill. He knows he can do it (positive self-efficacy)! He will, however, resist the more prestigious half-marathon because he doubts that he can complete the course in a 'respectable' time (negative self-efficacy).

Thus your level of motivation and performance in sport depends on what you think you can do rather than what indeed you can do. The same goes for teams. Self-efficacy in sport can be positively manipulated by your coach, and by your own mental attitudes in the following ways:

(a) **Previous experiences** – winning against that team again after a severe battle last season, confidence in running a sub-50 minute 10k in the city run after doing the same on the treadmill in the gym.

(b) **Modeling** – the person in your lane swims the 25-meter pool in 20 strokes, and you take 25. Watching her style persuades you that your stroke efficacy can also reach her standard.

(c) **Verbal persuasion** – someone who knows you well convinces you that you can take part in the sprint triathlon. You swim and run well, but you haven't biked since you were in the fifth grade.

(d) **How you interpret the feedback (emotional arousal):** you run the 10k and show a higher-than-expected pulse rate at the end of the event. You could attribute it to your doubting whether you are designed by nature to be a long-distance runner. Therefore you will not train for the half-marathon next season. Or you might attribute it to your feelings of excitement at your first long-distance run. So you will train for the half-marathon next season.

Roger Bannister ran the first-ever four-minute mile in 1954. Until then, many believed that the four-minute mile was a human impossibility. Within 18 months of Bannister's feat, 16 other athletes achieved the same thing.

The experimental work of Hochstetler et al (1985) focused on self-efficacy in women's cycling. 40 women took part, divided into two groups. The first group was shown a video of a woman doing a cycling task with great difficulty. The second group was shown a video of a woman doing the same task easily and effectively. Both groups then did the same cycling task. The first group had difficulty, but those in the second group took it in their stride – like the 'model' in the video.

Evaluation – the results suggest that modeling has a key role in self-efficacy-motivated achievement in sport. However, it was a controlled experiment, with the associated issue of ecological validity. Furthermore, the experiment was restricted to women, raising doubts of generalization to both genders.

Strengths of self-efficacy theory

(a) Studies, such as that of Hochstetler (above), have indicated that perceived self-efficacy is a good predictor of individual athletic performance.

(b) There is much anecdotal evidence from celebrities that attribute their sporting success to the forces that aroused their feeling of self-efficacy.

Limitations of self-efficacy theory

(a) Where studies are correlational, it is difficult to establish the cause-effect relationship between self-efficacy and improved sporting performance.

(b) Self-efficacy by itself does not take into account individual physiological factors. These might well be closer related to sporting success or lack of it.

Using one or more research studies, explain the role of goal-setting in the motivation of individuals.

The function of goal setting in sport is to raise motivation and performance. **Effective goals are:**

- Difficult, but possible to achieve.

- Clearly defined: exercising three times per week is less effective that swimming 60 lengths of the pool in 45 minutes every Sunday, Tuesday, and Friday.

- Inclusive of effective feedback mechanisms, focusing on progress to the goal.

Goals may be classified into:

(a) **Outcome goals** – such as an individual or team awards for winning a competition.

(b) **Performance goals** – such as completing a half-marathon in less than two hours.

(c) **Process goals** – such improving the swimming freestyle (front-crawl) stroke to reduce the number of strokes per 25-meter-pool-length; from 25 to 20.

Nicholls' achievement goal theory of motivation (1984) suggested that goals may be **task-goal orientated** (including the performance and process goals above) where you do not seek to outdo others, and **ego-goal orientated** where you do seek to outdo others – performance is judged on social comparison rather than on the standard achieved.

The experimental work of Filby et al (1999) examined the effectiveness of the different types of goal-setting on college-age soccer players. Players were divided into five groups. The first group had no goals. The second had outcome goals only – to win! The third had process goals only – to improve techniques of play. The fourth had both outcome and process goals. And the fifth had outcome, performance, and process goals.

The results showed that those without goals were the worst performers. The best performers were groups 4 and 5. Common to both of them were mixed task-goal orientated and ego-goal orientated targets. These incorporated both cognitive self-efficacy, and actual performance improvement.

Thus it appears that effective goal setting has the scope of focusing the athlete on goal-relevant activities, incorporating new and improved strategies into the existing skillset, increased self-efficacy, and overall increased motivation.

The experimental work of Schofield et al. (2005) investigated the efficacy of feedback strategies in motivating exercise-reluctant teenage girls in Australia. 85 girls took part in the study, and they were divided into three groups. Every girl in the first group received a pedometer (counts the number of steps taken), which could be set to register the number of paces towards a set daily target. Every girl in the second group was given time-based goals, which gave feedback about how long the particular activity was kept up. The third group - the control - was given no motivating strategies for improvement in sport.

The results showed an immediate improvement in fitness activity with the first group. The instant goal-related feedback from the pedometer was highly effective as a motivator, and in raising the girls' self-efficacy. The second group showed some progress after the twelfth week – the less effective time-based feedback having some effect. The goal-less third group showed no progress at all.

The results of this study indicate the importance of goal-setting with instant and effective feedback.

Discuss theories relating arousal and anxiety to performance *(for examples, optimal arousal theory/inverted U hypothesis, individual zone of optimal functioning theory).*

Athletes quite normally experience arousal and anxiety feelings. At top level where the competitors are pretty well matched, it is how they handle those feelings that can be the deciding factor in winning or losing.

Arousal is where perceived performance-stress activates the nervous system, the endocrine system, and the cardio-respiratory system. **Anxiety** involves the apprehension due to the associated state of arousal. Anxiety breaks down in to:

- Cognitive anxiety – doubts about self-efficacy, fear of failure.
- Somatic anxiety – uneasy feelings about the heightened physical arousal (above).
- State anxiety – severe apprehension at the beginning or at the climax of the event.
- Trait anxiety – some people are more inclined to apprehensive feelings than others, even in situations that are objectively non-threatening.

The combination of some pre-competitive arousal and anxiety can be an important motivator in sporting success. Too much can harm sporting performance.

*The Inverted U Hypothesis claims that there is an optimum level of biological (physiological) arousal for every task you do (Yerkes-Dodson Law, 1908). Too little, and you underperform. Too much, and you also underperform.

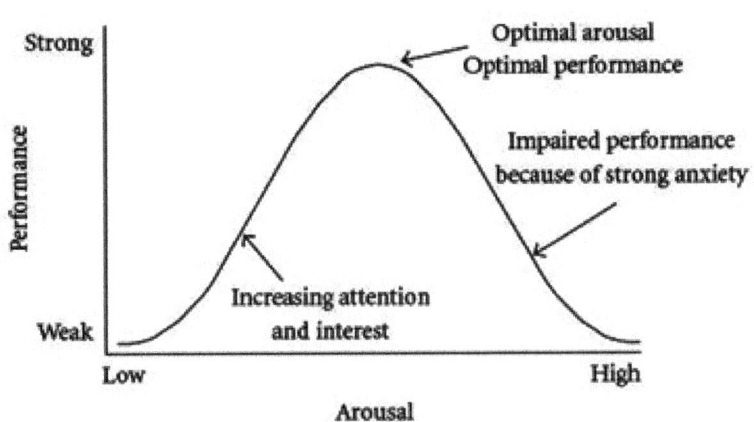

Generally, the more demanding the task, the higher is the optimum level of arousal.

Applying the inverted U hypothesis to sport, The work of Klavora (1998) applied the inverted U hypothesis to the pre-match anxiety of 95 male high-school basketball players in one season. The coaches judged the players' performance relative to their anxiety, which was measured by a standardized test. The results fitted in with the inverted U hypothesis. Those who performed best were in an optimum state of anxiety. Performance fell below top quality where players were both over-anxious and under-anxious.

Strengths of the Inverted U Hypothesis

1. The work of Klavora (above) does seem to indicate that there are optimum arousal levels, as presented by the inverted U.
2. It accepts that some anxiety is beneficial to optimize sporting performance.
3. It helps to account for elite sportspeople underperforming under high pressure.

Limitations of the Inverted U Hypothesis

1. Individuals vary in their optimum arousal levels.
2. Arousal is difficult to define and measure, especially when it depends on the self-reporting of the players.
3. Elite sportspeople tend to need greater levels of arousal to play to full potential than amateurs.

The Individual Zone of Optimal Functioning Theory (Hanin, 1997) holds that each person has his/her own optimum anxiety level. Everyone has their own individual and personal inverted U. It is the coach's job to get to know the players as individuals, and to discover the optimum point for each player. The coach then puts each sportsperson into an optimum personal level of arousal before the event.

Hanin also extended the theory to include positive emotions (like looking forward to being cheered for great play) as well as feelings of anxiety. Indeed, best performances combine optimum positive emotions with optimum negative emotions.

The work of Amnesi (1998) was a qualitative study involving three elite tennis players. The IZOF was established for each player. Then, each player measured their anxiety level before taking part in competitive events. They were then shown a technique to move that anxiety into their IZOF. The result was that all three players showed a distinct improvement in play.

Strengths of the IZOF Theory

1. It includes the notion that different persons have different inverted U curves.
2. The work of Hanin (above) shows that the IZOF theory can be applied effectively in a fully ecologically-valid real-life environment.
3. It focuses on positive emotions, as well as the feelings of anxiety that are characteristic in the application of the inverted U theory.

Limitations of the IZOF Theory

1. The AZOF of each individual is difficult and time-consuming to determine, especially when it depends on the self-reporting of the players.
2. Arousal is difficult to define and measure, especially when it depends on the self-reporting of the players.

SECTION TWO – SKILL DEVELOPMENT AND PERFORMANCE

Evaluate techniques for skill development used in sport

Massed practice versus distributive practice

Sports participants striving to improve need to incorporate various movements as part of their skill-set, such as spin-bowling in cricket, energy-efficient strokes in swimming, service-accuracy in tennis. Once the movement is mastered, it has to be integrated into the existing skillset, and practiced in order to reach 'fluent' expert performance, even when under pressure.

Practicing and developing new skills towards perfect standards may take the forms of:

- **(a) Massed practice** – where a specific skill is repeated over and over again without a break until it becomes 'fluent' and proficient. This is usually applied to a task which is discrete (a single unit of action with a clear start and finish), such as a serve in tennis, a penalty kick in soccer, or a spin-bowl in cricket.

- **(b) Distributed practice** – where a specific skill is developed by a series of exercises, such as to improve style in swimming, cycling, and running. Here, a practice session can involve watching a proficient athlete as a 'model', and then a series of varied exercises applying the skill, with tiredness-recovery rests in between. This is usually applied to a task which is continuous (a task that is not in single units, but may continue for as long as the participant wants).

- **(c) Variable practice** – where massed practice and distributed practice are combined. This is commonly used for development of skills which are repeated over and over again in an event – e.g. stroke perfection in swimming. Mass practice is applied to the movement involved in the actual stroke; distributed practice is applied to swimming more pool lengths incorporating that new skill.

The work of Singer (1965) compared the efficacy of massed practice and distributed practice. The specific task was bouncing a basketball off the floor and into the basket. Those in the first group repeated the exercise 80 times without a break (massed practice). Those in the second group took five minute breaks after every 20 shots (distributed practice). The third group carried out the task over a four-day period: 20 shots, then a 24-hour break (extended distributed practice).

All groups were tested twice, firstly immediately after the practice program, and finally a few days later. The results of the first test favored those in the extended distributed practice group. The results of the final test, however, seemed to favor the first two groups. This could have been because those first two groups had a chance to recover from the intensive practice in the time between the two tests.

Overall, massed practice seems to work best where the skill requires precision (e.g. a golf swing or a spin bowl) and the participant is well-motivated. Its constant repetition means that the athlete is more likely to remember the skill in the future (Singer). However, the repeated nature of the exercises can lead to boredom, and thus deter beginners.

Distributed practice works best where the player is at beginner standard, and where the energy required quickly creates fatigue. Being less intense, there is a greater chance that the skill will be forgotten after the training program.

Mental imagery is where the person imagines playing at his or her targeted standard, with eased proficiency in the necessary skills. This involves the details of the complex skillsets being fully activated in your mind's eye. Indeed, neuro-imaging indicates that the brain uses the same nerve mechanisms for imaginary movements as for actual movements. The brain does not tell the difference. The brain is thus in a state of functional equivalence.

Martin et al (1999) applied a SIQ (sport imagery questionnaire) framework for imagery research. Applied to triathlon (swimming/cycling/running) events for example, it would take the form of:

(i) Cognitive specific: the specific performance focus of "My mind's eye sees the image of my swimming with the perfect freestyle strokes."

(ii) Cognitive general: the general performance focus of "My mind's eye sees the image of my completing the sprint triathlon (swim 750 meters, bike 20 kilometers, run 5 kilometers) in under two hours."

(iii) Motivational specific: "My mind's eye seems me being cheered by my friends as I reach the finish."

(iv) Motivational arousal: when feeling anxious before the event: "My mind's eye sees me cool, and well psyched-up, but not over-psyched-up for the event. I'm ready to jump in the pool and swim out to the first buoy."

(v) Motivational general mastery: when feeling anxious before the event: "My mind's eye seems in full control of my breathing and heart rate."

The work of Callow and Hardy (2001) studied the performance of 123 elite netball players. Using the SIQ (based on self-reporting), the findings showed that netball players of different skills tended to use different types of imagery. Lower-skilled netballers with high confidence used motivational general mastery, and imagery related to the overall performance strategies (cognitive general). The higher-skilled players having high confidence tended to report on more goal-achievement-related images (cognitive specific, and motivational specific).

Overall, imagery has the benefit of allowing the sporting personality to mentally practice the moves just like when carrying them out in real life. Additional practice with thinking instead of

However, mental imagery has the weakness of being counterproductive. Those less confident can tune in to negative mental images (such as failing to complete the marathon), and underperform in consequence. It relies on athletes' self-reporting evidence, which is not always valid. Also, SIQs show that some sporting personalities do not use mental imaging at all, and seem to perform just as well without them.

To what extent does the role of coaches affect individual or team behavior in sport?

It is the coaches that not only teach the techniques of the game, but – most important – create the 'motivation atmosphere'. Part of your wishing to be part of the team includes your feelings of comfort with your coach. You like him/her, you feel he/she is on your side and is committed to your progress in the sport. So you will appreciate the feedback, even it is sternly disciplined and powerfully directed. You know that it is for your own good, because your objective and your coach's objective are one – your success in mastering the skill (performance goal) or winning the contest (outcome goal).

Indeed, the coach's job has been described by Short & Short (2005) as "teacher, organizer, competitor, learner, and friend/mentor."

You may feel less happy – and even drop out of the program completely, where the coach-created-atmosphere supports only the best participants, at the expense of the others (maybe including yourself). Where your long hours of devoted practice feel like you are bolstering up the coach's ego. Where his/her instructions are hard to follow, and you fear being shouted at because you were too shy and nervous to ask for clarification.

The work of Smith et al. (1979) emphasizes the following qualities that optimize effective coaching which encourage especially children to continue with the program and strive for constant improvement:
- (a) Rewarding effort in sport as well as achievement in sport.
- (b) Creating ways in which participants learn from their mistakes, instead of suffer for their mistakes.
- (c) Instructions and coach-expectations are communicated clearly.

The work of Fraser-Thomas et al. (2008) drew attention to the importance of teenagers feeling comfortable with their coach. This involved semi-structured interviews with two groups of teenagers; those who dropped out of coached swimming, and those who were continuing with coached swimming. Common to both groups was the experience of different styles of coaching and coaches' behavior. However, those who continued with the sport additionally reported a 'non-talking-down', positive working relationship with the coaches.

The work of Horn & Lox (1993) formulated the expectancy theory in sport, which created the four-step model to show how **performance in sport was a product of self-fulfilling prophecy:**

- (i) Coach communicates his/her expectations of the participant, on criteria such as appearance, past performance, skills, and tests.
- (ii) These expectations are the bases on which individual participants are treated by the coach. They affect the nature, quality, and manner of the feedback to participants.
- (iii) The feedback in turn influences the participants' future performance – positively or negatively, in tune with that feedback.
- (iv) That performance conforms to the original assessment and expectations of the coach, reinforcing the coach's initial assessment and expectations.

Indeed, the work of Chase et al. (1997) demonstrated that the same applied to teams as well as to individuals. Skill mastery was the element under the greatest influence of the coach, and it was that that was achievable by the participants. Focus on achievable performance goals avoided the danger of a coach's low efficacy expectation for the team, which could well lead to lower player efficacy when competing with other teams.

Explain relationships between team cohesion and performance.

Team cohesion enables the necessary cooperation to achieve the team goal of winning. It is the team sticking together. and remaining united in the pursuit of its goals and objectives. This involves **task cohesion** (where the team members work together to achieve common targets) and **social cohesion** (where the team members get on well with each other, and enjoy being together). Both are important.

Problems with team cohesion are evident, for example, in soccer. Player A will avoid taking the easy move of passing the ball to B, and opt for the much riskier option of passing it to C. His hostility towards B (either sportingly or personally) could mean that through him, the team lowers its chance of scoring that winning goal. Or perhaps A takes a long shot for goal, instead of passing to B or C. His ego wants the goal to be in his name. To serve the team, he is much better off simply kicking the ball to one of the other players positioned closer to the goalmouth.

Indeed, the degree of team cohesion depends on whether or not:

(a) The athlete is happy with being a member of the team.
(b) The athletes have a developed a history of working well together in previous team events.
(c) The team's interaction with the coach (see previous section) is mutually beneficial.
(d) The coaches need to be sensitive to the internal dynamics of the team. That is in order to facilitate an environment where participants interact positively and give support to each other.

The work of Paterson et al. (2005) looks at **productivity norms.** If the established productivity norm of the team is to strive hard to group success, appropriate cohesion will follow. Those who do not 'fit in' will not wish to remain in the team. They will leave. Paterson's work holds that it is the high productivity norm that influences team performance. Team cohesion is a bi-product of the norm, and also could be argued to be a product of past successful team performance.

In other words, good group cohesion is associated with team success, but it is difficult to establish the precise relationship because:

(a) It is not clear whether group cohesion is a cause of successful performance or an effect of successful performance (as above).
(b) It is impractical to set up a experiment with a suitable control that determines the cause and effect relationship.

As much of the research evidence is correlational, the question remains – **is it team cohesion that causes performance success, or is it performance success that causes team cohesion?**

Describe aids and barriers to team cohesion.

The following elements have been found to promote team cohesion:

(a) The stated goal of the team must be clear to the team and accepted by the team. If all members have that goal, all will strive together to achieve it.
(b) The team has a strong feeling of identity and purpose, and members feel good to belong to the team.
(c) The coach needs to sense the team climate and interact successfully with it. He/she understands/empathizes with the individuality of each of the group members, giving higher levels of training and positive feedback where necessary.

Barriers to team cohesion have been found to include:

(a) Poor communications between coach and team, and/or between members of the team.
(b) Lack of clarity and/or agreement between the coach and group members on the team's goals, and levels of training required to achieve them.
(c) Power-struggles and clashes of personalities within the team, or between the coach and a particularly dominant member of the team.
(d) Individual members feeling that they have not been given the positions in the team most suited to their abilities.

(e) High turnover of team players – reducing opportunities for members of the group to get to know one another and build up a cooperative sporting relationship.

Problems in sports - *this section tackles stress, injuries, burnout, and use of drugs in sport.*

Discuss athlete response to stress and chronic injury.

Stress and long-lasting (and even permanent) injuries are major hazards for a person in a sporting career, and for that matter an amateur for whom sporting activity is a way of life.

The work of Thatcher and Day (2008) conducted a series of semi-structured interviews with athlete trampolinists and found **the following stresses standing in the way of optimum sporting performance:**

(a) Surprise and uncertainty in the actual sporting event: unclear what precise skill(s) are being judged, larger number of competitors, not enough time to do the necessary warm-up exercises before the event, too much time before the event to avoid focus on the stiff competition.
(b) The position in the person's lifestyle – a surgeon who runs marathons will be concerned that the strains to complete in less than three hours will affect his efficacy at tomorrow's life-saving operation.
(c) An older athlete fears a possible injury that will bring his or her sporting career to a final termination.
(d) The sense of not being sufficiently prepared for the event – in terms of training, nutrition, and feeling overtired.

The work of Williams & Elliot (1999) shows that athletes do indeed respond to excessive anxiety levels in their facing greater risk of injury. For that anxiety causes both the visual perception, and the nervous system to be less accurate.

The work of Anderson and Williams (1999) was a quantitative study which determined the stress responses of some 200 athletes from 10 different sports in a laboratory situation. The determinants of stress were reaction times, visual perceptions, and anxiety levels. They also factored in the individual athletes' personal situations and degrees of social support. The findings about each athlete were combined to predict injuries during the season. The results showed that one combination of factors seemed to be positively correlated with stress-rooted likelihood of injury: major unpleasant life events (cognitive) together with low social support (socio-cultural) and narrowing of vision (biological) during laboratory tests in stress.

However, the work of Kaiseler et al. (2009) highlighted that the stress coping skills of individual athletes (mental toughness) varies a great deal, with many turning a stress or injury into an opportunity rather than as a threat.

Sporting injuries are most frequent in basketball, bicycling, and American football, with approximately half a million cases of each, as recorded in the USA National Electronic Surveillance System for the year 2006. These include eye and forehead injuries, fractured wrists, and broken legs. Indeed, the work of Finch (1998) indicates that about a quarter of all the injuries in the population are sports-related. That means that many athletes suffer the frustrations of long and painful rehabilitation.

Indeed, serious injury can devastate an athlete as it can mean the interruption and even the end of a promising sporting career. *The following two models give a framework for athletes' response to stress and injury:*

The grief-reaction-response model (Kubler-Ross, 1969) – as applied to sport psychology (Harris, 2003)

Kubler Ross' model is applied to the stages of becoming reconciled to the news that one is going to die from a terminal illness, which is first denial (It can't be!), then anger, then bargaining (trying to find a way out of the situation), then depression, and finally acceptance and reorganization of lifestyle. Applied to a serious sports injury:

(i) Denial – the athlete's initial reaction to the injury is just to play on.
(ii) Anger – when the athlete realizes the consequences in terms of earning power, career prospects, and status as a sporting celebrity.
(iii) Bargaining – seeking in vain to find a short cut to return to the sport.
(iv) Depression – as rehabilitation takes its time or clearly will never be complete.
(v) Acceptance and reorganization – where the athlete fully comes to terms with the realities of the situation.

Strengths of the grief-reaction-response model

1. It indicates a range of factors that combine to enable the athlete to cope with the injury.
2. It is widely accepted by coaches as a means of understanding the athlete's way of coping with injury.

Limitations of the grief reaction response model

1. The original model was focused on the human life cycle rather than on sports injuries.
2. Lacks empirical support – the evidence of the model working is largely anecdotal, relying on self-reporting.
3. The work of Udry (1997) indicated minimal evidence for the first stage (denial), and none for the third stage (bargaining).

Indeed, the work of Petipas & Danish (1995) indicates that the element of sporting loss of identity is a crucial element arising from a serious sports injury. Such a person feels that he or she is not the same person if unable to play and compete.

The cognitive appraisal model (Udry et. al, 1997)

A professional soccer player suffers a dislocated hip, following an unsuccessful tackle. His series of appraisals listed below enables him to come to terms with his new reality as the sufferer of a severe sports injury:

(i) The injury happened. No going back. No more football this season.
(ii) The appraisal. How bad is the injury? Is it as bad as last time (if there had been a 'last time')? Or as bad as X-in-the-team's hip dislocation? That involves the athlete's subjective perception of the problem, which could have little resemblance to the actual severity of the injury.
(iii) The emotional response, which could be much greater or much less than the situation indicates.
(iv) The coping response, adapting to the injury's pain and inconvenience.
(v) Following the rehabilitation program, and adapting to it through a further series of appraisals in the light of further improvements and setbacks.

Strengths of the cognitive appraisal model

1. Flexible – allows for a very wide spectrum of athletes' personality types, including the notion that the athlete tied his personality to the sport.
2. The model can incorporate the crucial situational and dispositional factors involved in the athlete coming to terms with the injury.
3. It can accommodate breakdowns in the final stage, where for example an athlete misses a treatment installment and faces a rapid deterioration in the rehabilitation process.

Limitations of the cognitive appraisal model.

1. It does not readily accommodate the situation of chronic injury – where full recovery may never happen.
2. It needs to take into account that the athlete might continue with the sport despite the injury. The pain suffered is more endurable than having to drop out of the sport.

Examine the reasons for using drugs in sports.

The reality is that athletes' determination to shine has involved some of them using unfair means, including drugs. The World Anti-Doping Agency reports that about 1% of athletes test positive for a banned drug. This can go up to 7% with high-level athletes, and very much higher in some sports such as cycling and weightlifting. Indeed, the high pressure to win is likely to account for the higher figure with high-level, elite, athletes.

The pressures that athletes face may incline them towards using drugs. This is despite the risk of severe medical consequences including addiction, dishonesty, bringing a bad name to the sport, and suspension (or worse) from play. The pressures include:

(a) Biological – the attitude that taking drugs enhances performance: amphetamines keep up the high energy levels for cycling, anabolic steroids for weightlifting, beta-blockers to control fine-muscle movements.
(b) Biological – to cope with pain and injury rehabilitation, including narcotics such as heroin.
(c) Biological – to develop a more sporting-looking body: anabolic steroids are used to increase muscle size and strength.
(d) Cognitive – the use of beta-blockers to control anxiety and stress.
(e) Cognitive – to satisfy the notion that drugs make it possible to break a world record and enter the halls of fame.
(f) Cognitive – accepting the framework that everybody has equal access to drugs, the competition opposition also takes drugs, the chances of getting caught (with severe consequences to reputation and future career) are very slim and well-worth the risks of the random checks.
(g) Cognitive – the attitude that 'if everyone does it, why should only I suffer disadvantage by not taking any?'
(h) Socio-cultural – young athletes are more likely to turn to drugs to enhance sporting performance if they see their older role models doing the same thing (social learning theory).
(i) Socio-cultural – huge sums of money for winning, availability of public and private financial support being dependent on high performance, pressure from coaches, spectators, family, and friends.
(j) Socio-cultural – the conviction of drug use in elite swimmers representing China at international levels in the 1990s raised the notion that athletes' drug use was considered the norm in some cultures. To win by any means was the sole goal.

Discuss the effects of drug use in sport.

Review the material in the above list, for use in this section.

The high risk of physiological damage and also being caught has not deterred athletes, and especially elite athletes, from taking drugs. In terms of actual and perceived benefits:

(a) Anabolic steroids increase the number of oxygen-carrying red blood cells, and muscle size and strength – particularly relevant to sports such as discus, shot-put, and weightlifting. The dangers are severe interference with primary and secondary sexual characteristics (males: sterility, increase in breast size, and sterility; females: interference with the menstrual cycle, enlarged clitoris, facial hair), and also mood-swings and aggressive feelings. The extreme case is that of international shot-out champion Heidi Krieger (then of East Germany) who was deceived by her coaches in taking anabolic steroids. She already appeared masculine by age 18, and only discovered that she had been regularly taken-in by her coaches following the severe back and joints pains which caused the termination of her sporting career. Following severe depression, she eventually had a gender change and is now Andreas Krieger.

(b) Beta-2-agonists, like anabolic steroids, also increase muscle size. As water-soluble tablets, they have the additional advantage of being detectable for a shorter period of time in the body, making it less likely to get caught. Amongst their long-term effects are cancer of the liver and the kidneys.

The work of Bloodworth and McNamee (2010) involved a focus group interview of British athletes to determine the most effective deterrents to the use of drugs in sport. It showed that the most effective one was the notion that taking drugs for sporting success would reduce life expectancy by 10 years. It was far more effective than the risks of the inevitable consequences of being discovered having taken drugs to enhance sporting and competitive performance.

Compare models of causes and prevention of burnout *(for example, cognitive-affective stress model, investment/entrapment model).*

Burnout is likely to occur in many areas of life. It follows prolonged, intense activity – whether at work, in study (beware that you pace organize your IB studies so that you avoid burnout), or simply taking on too much over a long period.

When burnt-out, you withdraw from a formerly stimulating and/or enjoyable activity in response to chronic stress and loss of interest.

Applied to sport, the burnout scenario can typically affect an athlete after (for example) years of daily swimming practice. Length after length against time, staring at the line at the bottom of the pool builds up chronic stress. He or she wants to avoid the pool altogether, consistently underperforms, and misses a swim meet on the slightest pretext. The sport becomes a source of boredom and even torment, rather than one of challenge and self-fulfillment.

The cognitive-affective model (Smith, 1986) views burnout as a response to chronic stress, typically caused by regular overtraining over a long period. It is a progressive condition with four identifiable stages:

(i) High pressure to win or reach target level of achievement, leading to chronic stress. The stresses can be from parents and coaches, or from the athlete striving for perfection (Gould et. al. 1996-7).
(ii) Feelings of distress and even helplessness when appraising the situation (subjectively, and not necessarily realistically).
(iii) Paying attention to his/her biological responses, such as insomnia, weakened immune system, and tiredness.
(iv) Behavior in relationship to the biological responses: poorer athletic performance and difficulties in personal relationships.

This model may be applied to prevent burnout – by incorporating stress-management techniques such as social support and MSBR (see chapter 6, health psychology), and allowing more time between training sessions. These can get to the roots of the accumulating chronic stress.

In the first stage of the model, the high pressure to perform might be identified with the feeling of losing social life and lack of other interests. It may be applied to the prevention of burnout by encouraging the athlete to take time off, sleep more hours, turn to more relaxing activities (such as 'hanging out' with friends, going to see a movie), and restructuring the way of looking at things through cognitive therapy.

Strengths of the cognitive-affective model

(a) May be applied to detect and reverse burnout, from its early stages, e.g. when the athlete uses avoidance strategies as coping mechanisms.
(b) Supported by empirical evidence – of athletes using avoidance strategies as coping mechanisms, of feeling trapped in the sport, and of feeling that other elements of life are just passing by.

Limitations of the cognitive-affective model.

(a) It treats stress as cause of burnout, rather than as a symptom of burnout. Thus stress might not be a mere warning of oncoming burnout, but a sign of arrival at the burnout stage.
(b) Needs to incorporate how hardy the suffering athlete is.

The investment/entrapment model (Raedeke, 1997) is a cognitive model that involves the athlete's appraisal of his/her position. The central issue is: "Is it worth it?" In contrast to the cognitive-affective model, **burnout comes together with the athlete's realization that all the efforts put into the chosen sport are not worth the investment of time and energy.**

The typical burnout symptom according to this model is withdrawal and showing dislike for the sport.

The work of Raedeke (1997) looked at the reasons elite athletes were involved in the sport: enthusiasm or entrapment? A sample of over 200 teenage elite swimmers of both sexes responded to a questionnaire that assessed the factors determining commitment on one side and burnout on the other. Those swimmers who reported have been 'entrapped' in taking part scored higher on burnout scores than those who felt 'enthused' in taking part. The work concluded that feeling entrapped was a characteristic of burnout: they would like to get out of the sport if they could.

This model may be applied to prevent burnout – by incorporating problem-solving techniques, and allowing more time between training sessions.

Entrapment may also be taken into account with coaching strategies. That would include a varied and exciting training program, the setting of realistic and achievable targets, and a supporting coaching atmosphere that promotes friendship and cohesion within the group. These would strive to maintain the atmosphere of commitment and enthusiasm.

Strengths of the investment/entrapment model

(a) Introduces the notion of entrapment – that burnout occurs because the athlete feels he or she is locked into a physically and mentally demanding program that does not seem to be worth the investment in time or effort.
(b) May be applied to detect and reverse burnout from its early stages, e.g. when the athlete uses avoidance strategies as coping mechanisms.

Limitations of the investment/entrapment model

(a) The feeling of entrapment may be a byproduct of the high pressure to cope with stress, rather than a carefully weighed-up appraisal of the situation. It is not the only cause of burnout, and it is likely to be operating with other equally important factors, such as the stress caused by the intensive levels of training.
(b) The difficulties of performing controlled investigations of entrapment raise the question as to how far indeed entrapment is a cause of burnout – the difficulty of determining cause and effect.

POSSIBLE EXAMINATION QUESTIONS

LONG ANSWER QUESTIONS ONLY ON PAPER TWO

Using one or more research studies, explain the role of goal-setting in the motivation of individuals.

Evaluate techniques for skill development used in sport

Compare and contrast models of causes and prevention of burnout in sport

---

CHAPTER NINE – QUALITATIVE METHODOLOGY IN PSYCHOLOGY

Paper 3

The chapter below assumes that you have studied the material in class. It should help to sort the ideas out into a semblance of order for revision purposes.

General characteristics and issues with qualitative research in psychology

Qualitative researchers aim to gather an in-depth understanding of human behavior and the factors that influence behavior.

Qualitative research strategies include the use of observations, interviews and case studies – typically in a natural setting. These are the foci of this unit.

Qualitative research often involves face-to-face interactions between researcher and participant, where the researcher needs to tune in and adjust to the social context within which the data is obtained. The data then undergoes analysis and interpretation, which typically enables themes, categories or theories to emerge from the data,

Sampling methods used in qualitative research tend to be different to those used in quantitative research (the methods you practiced for your internal assessment investigation). Purposive sampling rather than random sampling is preferred in qualitative research; participants (and that can include a single participant in a case study) are often selected for having the characteristics that fit in with the research aim. How far the findings of qualitative studies may be generalized to similar situations outside the study has to be carefully assessed in each investigation.

Credibility improves when researchers are reflexive; they attempt to make readers of their research aware of their own potential researcher bias.

Qualitative and quantitative research complement each other. They may both be used in one focus of psychological study.

In the Paper III one-hour examination, you will be given an unseen piece of research and three short answer questions (SAQ), each taking 10 marks. These questions will require you to apply your knowledge of the nature, applications, and limitations of qualitative techniques to the research presented.

Treat the qualitative techniques below as tools to be applied to an unseen psychology scenario. Make sure you know their merits and limitations.

A. Theory and practice in qualitative research

Distinguish between qualitative and quantitative data.

Quantitative data is in the form of 'numbers' that are readily summarized and subjected to statistical analysis and tests. Quantitative data is meant for generalization beyond the sample from which the data was drawn.

Qualitative data comes from interaction with participants – e.g. interviews, field observations. The data is 'text rich' – open-ended responses that are open to different interpretation. Analysis may be based on existing theory, or on theory emerging from observed patterns within the data.

Explain the strengths and limitations of a qualitative approach to research.

STRENGTHS

1. Adaptable to investigating complex and sensitive issues – e.g. living in a violent relationship.
2. Provides in-depth experience of interest to the psychologist not easily obtained by quantitative methods.
3. Help to explain phenomena – e.g. why relationships break up.
4. Identifies and evaluates factors that may contribute to solving a problem – e.g. what initiatives would help couples sustain their relationships.
5. Ecological validity – participants respond in the context of their own environment.

WEAKNESSES

1. Long interviews and observations are time-consuming.
2. May generate large amounts of data, making it difficult to identify patterns.
3. Problems in data analysis being reflexive (influenced by the viewpoint of the researcher), as it lacks the impartial quantitative, statistical framework.

To what extent can findings be generalized from qualitative studies?

The small number of participants means that the findings may not easily be generalized to situations similar to the study (representational generalization weaknesses), and to those in different settings from the study (inferential representation weaknesses).

For example, if the study of homelessness was made in London, it would be harder to transfer the conclusions of the study to a medium-sized community such as Liverpool, where the homeless person is less likely to be a newcomer and more likely to be personally known to others in that community. However, if evidence from other studies confirms the findings, there is greater scope for generalization.

Discuss ethical considerations in qualitative research.

These always have to be taken into consideration in carrying out qualitative research. They are likely to be included in any examination response involving choice and justification of specific methods.

Generally, but not always similar to the ones you might have used in your quantitative research. These include:

1. Informed consent – participants must know the object of the study, that their involvement is voluntary, and what the data will be used for. In extreme cases, the ethical requirement for informed consent (which may be withdrawn/renegotiated through the study) might be waived. That includes where covert observation is the only practical way to obtain the necessary information that is vital to public welfare. For example, to prevent faulty diagnosis of individuals as suffering from mental diseases when they are mentally healthy (e.g. Rosenhan, 1974 – chapter 4).

2. Protecting participants from harm – bearing in mind that if abuse, or sexual behavior is the area studied, the participant might be disclosing the information for the first time. He or she might initially feel comfortable with the researcher. However there might be remorse, or at least second thoughts later on. A situation has to be avoided where the participant will subsequently regret having shared the vital, highly-sensitive information before having got to know the researcher well enough to be comfortable with him/her.

3. Issues of anonymity and confidentiality may arise in case studies because of the risk of identification. Minor details in the report may have to be changed.

Discuss sampling techniques appropriate to qualitative research *(for example, purposive sampling, snowball sampling)*.

1. Purposive sampling – participants are selected because their particular situation fits in with the research topic. If the topic is divorce, those in the sample are likely to be contemplating divorce, or are divorced. Advantages – can obtain information quickly as the sample is already filtered. Disadvantages – can still be unwanted diversity within the sample (e.g. participants of different cultures), and the sample may be biased because of its small size.

2. Snowball sampling – where the researcher asks the participants if he knows other people in a similar situation. Advantages – can be cost effective, and quick access to those who otherwise might be hard to find. Disadvantages – it is difficult to avoid bias in the sample (as related to those who the initial participant knows), and there could be ethical concerns of confidentiality (due to the manner in which the participants would have been recruited).

3. Convenience sampling – where the sample is restricted to those who would like to take part, typically through advertizing or a notice in university psychology department or the student union. Advantages and disadvantages – similar to #2 above.

Explain effects of participant expectations and researcher bias in qualitative research.

Participant expectations are like demand characteristics – the participant may feel that being frank will cause a negative reaction. S/he will give the response which will appear to please the researcher

Researcher bias can be explained by the researcher not paying enough attention to the participants, so it is the researcher's own beliefs (self-serving bias) that determine the recording and the interpretation of the findings. This element might be factored in by asking the participants to comment on the researcher's observations.

Explain the importance of credibility in qualitative research.

Credibility of a qualitative study may be established by the participants leaving a decision trail (through a suitable list of references) so that the reader would be able to track and verify the research process. This transparency would increase the study's credibility.

Qualitative researchers improve their credibility by the practice of peer review – sharing their findings with other researchers in the field.

Explain the effect of triangulation on the credibility/trustworthiness of qualitative research.

Triangulation involves researching the same issue by more than one method, as the findings from one procedure serve as a check on the findings from the other procedure. Method triangulation involves comparing data from different methods – e.g. quantitative and qualitative. Data triangulation involves comparing data gathered from other participants, sources, or different qualitative methods (e.g. observations and interviews). Researcher triangulation involves the use of several observers, interviewers, or researchers to compare and check data collection and interpretation.

It has the advantage of being a means of checking on the findings of the application of method. However, it is still questioned by radical quantitative psychologists on the grounds that qualitative research can never be entirely free from bias.

Explain reflexivity in qualitative research.

Reflexivity that the researcher needs to reflect on his or her own background and beliefs, and how these could influence the research process. It acknowledges that background and beliefs can influence the way research is conducted and findings can be interpreted. This line of thinking means that researchers should provide sufficient details about issues that might bias the investigation – e.g. cultural background.

Reflexivity can be personal (as explained above), or epistemological (related to the method information has been 'traditionally' obtained by previous psychological research in that field).

B. Interviews

Evaluate semi-structured, focus group and narrative interviews.

Semi-structured interviews involve the preparation of a list of bases that must be covered – which typically use closed and open-ended questions. The closed questions get the participant to talk in a focused way, and the open ones enable him/her to expand and respond more freely. Open-ended questions tend reveal deeper insights of the person's experiences of what is being investigated.

STRENGTHS

- Enables researcher to intervene, asking participants for clarification/expansion.
- Allows for pursuing themes that arise in the interview.
- Compatible with many types of data analysis.

LIMITATIONS

- The typically formal nature of the interview raises issues of ecological validity.
- Data obtained on this basis can be extensive and cumbersome to analyze.

Focus groups – typically consist of a group of 6-10 people where the researcher acts as facilitator. The researcher introduces the issue, and directs / monitors the discussion.

STRENGTHS

- Enables data to be collected from several people together.
- More natural setting – higher ecological validity.

LIMITATIONS

- Not suited to all issues, especially personal ones that people shy from discussing in company.
- Presence of others may bring group conformity, as with the Asche paradigm (chapter 3).

Narrative interviews – researchers discover how the participants make sense of events in their lives by analyzing the details and structure of the ways that they talk about them. This is used to explore the meanings and cultural contexts of those events. It could be used in a study on what it is like to be a new student at the school.

The narrative interview could be on the lines of: "tell me what you thought when you were put in the situation and how you coped with it". The respondents might focus on the coping mechanisms, and what changes the experience gave to their overall ways of coping with the stress.

STRENGTHS

- Enables people to talk freely.
- Content of information shows up elements of importance and meaning to the participants.

LIMITATIONS

- May contain a great deal of data of little value.
- Very time-consuming to process the data.

Discuss considerations involved before, during and after an interview *(for example, sampling method, data recording, traditional versus postmodern transcription, debriefing).*

Considerations before an interview:

(a) Interviewers must be suited for their task – such as being of an appropriate age, gender, and ethnicity. Must be able to establish rapport with respondent - towards a trusting and open working relationship.
(b) Suitable interview guidance – to some degree scripted, but also guidelines as how to adjust the questions to the respondent (typically including a range of open-ended questions).
(c) Be aware that note-taking can interfere with eye-contact. Audio/video recording might make the participant feel awkward, and adversely affect the authenticity of interview data. To avoid that problem, it is necessary to explain the objectives of the research in advance and offer the respondent a transcript of the interview as debriefing.

Considerations during an interview:

(a) Need to avoid anything (e.g. handling of recording equipment) interfering with the necessary eye contact required in the interview.
(b) Active listening – summarize and restate the respondents' views in different words. Pick up on them later, where relevant.
(c) Interview must avoid significant "interview effect" such as unconscious non-verbal communication (e.g. a smile) suggesting the type of response that the interviewer wants.
(d) Tackling the reflexivity issue – e.g. if the study is of the homeless, the interview may want to reveal that s/he once had been a homeless university student.

Considerations after an interview:

(a) Decide whether the transcript should be word for word (verbatim transcript), or needs to include pauses, change in facial expression, false starts, laughter (postmodern transcript).
(b) Debriefing – explain to participant how information might be used, and that confidentiality and all other ethical considerations will be observed.
(c) Recognition that the respondent might regret having divulged sensitive information and wishes to withdraw those elements for use by the researcher.

Explain how researchers use inductive content analysis on interview transcripts.

Inductive content analysis is the use of classification codes to reduce volumes of recorded material into more manageable (typically hierarchically-structured) data from which researchers identify patterns and gain insight. Inductive content analysis arrives at meanings that are **drawn out** of the data that is provided by the interviewee. It differs from a deductive approach where the researcher will have a pre-existing theoretical framework to accommodate the participant's response.

This qualitative method enables researchers to analyze materials in areas in which only limited knowledge exists, and thus the focus is on what emerges from that data.

Inductive content analysis may be carried out by **IPA (interpretative phenomenological analysis),** typically involving:

- Working through the transcripts.
- Identifying emergent themes.
- Deciding how those themes relate to each other through placing them in clusters and hierarchies (e.g. effect of the birth of a new child in the family would be a "new baby" cluster).
- Producing a summary table of the themes and relevant details according to the interviewed participant(s).

STRENGTHS

- Includes the scope for analyzing non-verbal, as well as verbal communication – with the use of postmodern transcripts.
- Allows sufficient flexibility for the researcher to view relationships not envisaged at the time of planning the research.

LIMITATIONS

- Reflexivity issue - problem of determining how far the findings are actually grounded in the data rather than in the researcher's personal situation.
- Need to compare with previous research on the issue.

C. Observations

Evaluate participant, non-participant, naturalistic, overt and covert observations.

Observation involves the viewing of naturally occurring behavior. It allows for ecological validity – a natural environment and thus natural behavior. There exists the compromise between the level of intervention of the researcher, and the validity of the results beyond the specific observational setting. Such research is also almost certainly going to be more realistic where the observer is unaware of being observed. The types of observation methods include:

Participant observations – involve the researcher becoming involved in the everyday life of the subjects. It may be overt (with the group's knowledge) or covert (without the group's knowledge). Covert participant observation is exemplified by the work of Festinger (1956). This studied the way of life of a group which believed that the world was coming to an end on December 31st of that year. Those following the group's rituals, texts and ideologies would rescued by a flying saucer. Data for this study was obtained by participant observation, where the researcher became involved in the everyday life of those being observed.

.STRENGTHS

- Brings the researcher closer to the phenomena investigated, enabling higher levels of disclosure of information relevant to reasons and motivation for their behavior (likely to be more in covert than overt).
- Potential for the above to yield a very detailed in-depth knowledge (likely to be more in covert than overt).

LIMITATIONS

- Difficulties in recording data promptly and objectively (likely to be greater in covert than overt).
- Ethical issues in covert (and sometimes overt as well) of deceiving participants of the true purpose of the study, which can only be justified ethically if the investigation is of high public importance and no other suitable method is available.
- Potentially dangerous when investigating the behavior of street gangs and drug pushers.

Non-participant observation: naturalistic observations – involve the recording of spontaneously occurring behavior in the subject's own natural environment. This is exemplified by the study of Ainsworth (1967, see chapter 5), where she explored the relationship between the degree of the baby's attachment to the mother on one hand, and (i) the maternal sensitivities to the baby's signals (based on interview data), (ii) the amount of holding by the mother (based on naturalistic observations in living rooms, for two hours at a time over a nine-month period) on the other. The findings were recorded on semantic scales, and those factors were found to be positively correlated.

STRENGTHS

- High ecological validity of observed behavior.
- Participants are unaware or at least indifferent to being observed, so demand characteristics are not an issue.

LIMITATIONS

- Causation is difficult to establish - cannot legitimately infer cause-and-effect relationships between variables that are only controlled, but not manipulated.
- Potential of interference from extraneous variables – 'atypical' behavior may not be recognized as such by the observer.
- Potential ethical issues of invasion of privacy.

(You may refer to the use of observation techniques within the St. Helena effect-of-television-on-violence study of 1995, in chapter 3)

Discuss considerations involved in setting up and carrying out an observation *(for example, Hawthorne effect, Rosenthal effect).*

It is important that the observer(s) are familiar with the context and the people they are observing, which could reduce some of the problems inherent in being a stranger in the setting. Additional considerations to take into account are:

- Hawthorne effect – where behavior of those observed changes significantly from the norm due to their knowing that they are being watched. It has been used to explain an increase of the workers' activity when they know that they are being looked over by people that 'matter'.
- Rosenthal effect – where the researcher comes to the investigation with preconceived idea, leading to credibility issues of a biased analysis of the data.

All the above can adversely affect ecological validity. Concerns over the Rosenthal effect may be met by having several observers working at the same time.

Discuss how researchers analyze data obtained in observational research

One well-established method is **grounded theory analysis.** This involves an inductive approach to data analysis – the creation of a picture as the data is collected and examined. The core approach of grounded theory analysis is based on:

(a) A full description of the phenomenon studied, and what has been picked up in the observation process.
(b) Classification of the notes into themes and subthemes relevant to the research, coded and arranged hierarchically.
(c) Interpretation of data, plus elements to both support and question the proposal.
(d) Producing an account based on all the elements of the analysis. This includes a theoretical framework for understanding the phenomenon under investigation. The theoretical explanation is 'grounded' – based on the categories identified during the observation. The researcher may follow-up contact with those observed for confirmation/negation of the analysis from the findings, and/or may compare with the findings from other researchers in the field for credibility.

It goes further than content analysis, in that the final product is indeed a written account based on all the elements of the analysis - a theoretical framework in which to place the phenomena studied.

STRENGTHS

- Enables researcher to follow-up, asking participants for clarification/expansion.
- Allows for pursuing themes that arise in the interview; those not prepared in advance.
- Compatible with many methods of data analysis.

LIMITATIONS

- Potential of interference from extraneous variables – 'atypical' behavior may not be recognized as such by the observer, as in the Hawthorne effect.
- Potential ethical issues of invasion of privacy.

D. Case studies

Evaluate the use of case studies in research

Area of research – is there a critical age for language learning?

This approach is exemplified in **seeking to discover the critical age for language learning – with Curtiss' study of Genie (1977)**. Genie was an American child raised in conditions of extreme deprivation until her discovery in 1970 at the age of 13 years and 7 months. Among other appalling treatment, Genie was beaten if she made any noise, and had learnt to suppress almost all vocalizations, except for a whimper. According to Curtiss, Genie was 'un-socialized, primitive, and hardly human'. Though she could understand a handful of words, she essentially had to learn her first language at the age of 14. The case study showed that she never developed normal language skills, and by age 18, she could only produce short sentences that were grammatically incorrect – including incorrect use of pronouns. Her vocabulary subsequently expanded, but her intonation remained comprehensible to only those who knew her, and Genie herself had great difficulty in understanding complex syntax. The fact that Genie could learn any language at all weakens Lenneberg's claim (1967) that there is a critical age-bound period for language learning. However, her obvious linguistic retardation is consistent with the existence of a **sensitive period for language learning**. As Schaffer (2004) writes, the 'safe and not very startling conclusion" is that, "...childhood is the optimal period for language learning. There is... flexibility in the precise age... and there is also no definite evidence supporting Lenneberg's contention that puberty is the point beyond which any further learning becomes possible".

Strengths of Case Studies.

- Highly detailed and in-depth; 'data-thick'.
- High ecological validity of data obtained.
- Enables insight into the social processes operating in a group (e.g. Festinger 1956).
- Often the only method suitable for studying specific learning processes – e.g. the acquisition of human language in primates.
- Often the only method suitable for studying some rare forms of behavior – e.g. Curtiss' study of Genie (above).

Limitations of Case Studies.

- Not always easy to distinguish cause and effect.
- Inferential generalization: single cases have problems when applied to the general population.
- Issue of reflexivity – researcher bias.
- Difficult or even impossible to replicate.

Explain how a case study could be used to investigate a problem in an organization or group *(for example, a football team, a school, a family).*

Example: "Can specific coaching strategies used by a soccer coach promote motivation and build self-efficacy in a team with a high turnover rate?"

The design would focus on one coach who currently has a large amount of contact time with a non-cohesive and poorly-motivated team. Data collection could be based on participant observation, and semi-structured interviews of the coach and members of the team - data triangulation in the study.

The team could be videoed for further analysis. The coach should be known as efficient, and there should be a relatively high number of new players in the team. The researcher could be a participant observer serving as assistant-coach during the observation.

Different types of coaching strategies would need to be observed from the same coach, with appropriate field notes taken. The observed players' reactions are followed up with semi-structured interviews.

The findings from the data analysis could apply IPA / grounded theory for confirming existing theory (e.g. mental imagery as a motivator theory, see Chapter 8), and/or developing new theory.

The conclusions would lead to recommendations for various coaching strategies more suitable for disaffected teams – e.g. greater focus on achievable targets, involvement of players in target setting, and in improving communication between the team and coach.

The findings should be followed up with further cases studies, indicating the degree of generalization that might be valid from this study.

Discuss the extent to which findings can be generalized from a single case study.

Extreme quantitative psychologists argue that case studies have little validity outside the case itself, as they lack empirical support.

Qualitative psychologists claim that as long as the study is supported by evidence from similar other ones, it may be possible to generalize to other people who are similar to those in the case study. If the patterns found in a single case study replicate the pattern found in other case studies, the theory derived from the single case study gains in applicability.

Findings from a case study may contradict common beliefs (e.g. that of Lenneberg in the Genie study, above), despite generalization problems.

A case study's scope for application to similar situations may be enhanced by considering the similarity of the relevant parts of the 'data-rich' material used to extrapolate its grounded theory. This is referred to as the case study's 'transferability'.

PAPER THREE-TYPE EXAMINATION QUESTION

The stimulus material below is based on a research article

Bullying is where a person is repeatedly exposed to intentional negative actions from one or more people. It may be physical, verbal, or psychological. Not all bullying is overt, but can build up through a series of separate incidents. It is traditionally associated with schools, but may also happen wherever people regularly gather together, including the workplace.

The research of Mishna et al (2005) recognized from previous studies that school-teachers do not consistently intervene to stop bullying. The study aimed to determine the extent that teachers understand the nature of bullying in their schools, what factors might influence their recognition of bullying, and their response to it.

Children in four city public schools of different socio-economic levels completed surveys about their experience with bullying. 17 children self-reported themselves as being frequently bullied. A total of 13 teachers were interviewed about those 17 children in their classrooms who self-identified as being frequently bullied. The semi-structured interviews lasted from one hour to two-and-half hours, depending on how many bullied children were in a particular teacher's class. Teachers were asked about their response to a child reporting being bullied, their general pattern of interactions with the child (and parent, if applicable), and the school's capacity to respond to bullying.

The teacher responses showed that they did not know that 10 of the 17 children had been bullied. Of the seven children – less than half the total - whom the teachers knew about, five had been helped by a teacher in a variety of ways.

These semi-structured interviews highlighted how teachers identified and handled incidents of bullying. Whilst there was agreement over physical aggression, some tended to take verbal and psychological bullying less seriously. Some teachers also considered the behavior of individual bullied children as responsible for their being bullied.

The findings of this qualitative study showed most of the teachers had neither been trained on dealing with bullying, nor had expressed the desire for such training. It also showed that teachers who would express empathy for others would be more likely to report and follow through with incidents of bullying.

Answer all the following three questions.

1. Discuss the considerations involved before, during, and after the interviews. *(10 marks)*

2. How might inductive content analysis be applied to the transcripts of the teachers' responses? *(10 marks)*

3. Explain how issues of reflexivity may have been handled in this study. *(10 marks)*

A-Z CHECKLIST FOR YOUR INTERNAL ASSESSMENT (Higher Level)

As this is a revision book, check that your experimental study:

(a) Is indeed experimental – it must be controlled.
(b) Does not involve the participation of animals.
(c) Does not involve children substantially younger than yourselves.
(d) Does not involve the ingestion or any other use of substances.
(e) Incorporates relevant theory and/or research studies as relevant background study.
(f) Has a clearly justified simple positive and null hypothesis. The justification should come from the background studies and/or the theories.
(g) Identifies independent and dependent variables.
(h) Shows which ethical guidelines are relevant, and describes how they will be followed.
(i) Identifies the characteristics of the sample population.
(j) Uses a large enough sample to apply statistical methods
(k) Justifies the means of sample selection.
(l) Clearly describes the experimental procedure.
(m) Contains evidence of following ethical guidelines during the experimental procedure.
(n) Refers to materials used (e.g. the debriefing statement), which are included in the appendix.
(o) States the results clearly, appropriately, and accurately graphed. The results address the hypothesis of the research.
(p) Applies appropriate descriptive statistics, including one measure of central tendency (e.g. mode, median, and mean) and one measure of dispersion (e.g. standard deviation).
(q) Applies an appropriate inferential statistical test (e.g. chi square, t-test).
(r) Includes a clear statement of statistical significance.
(s) Explicitly accepts or rejects the null hypothesis, on the basis of the inferential statistic.
(t) Evaluates the results in the light of the acceptance or rejection of the null hypothesis.
(u) Evaluates the results in the light of previously incorporated background theory and/or research studies.
(v) Considers limitations of the design and procedures, and suggests ideas for further relevant research.
(w) Ends with an appropriate conclusion.
(x) Includes in-text referencing where relevant, and an appendix with a bibliography, briefing and debriefing statements, and sample questionnaire / illustrations used.
(y) Includes a title page and a clearly written abstract.
(z) Is between the word limits of 1,500 and 2,000.

AND FINALLY REMEMBER

Paper 1 – Core exam paper. Three compulsory short-answer question, one optional long answer question. Chapters 1, 2, and 3 of this book. Two hours.

Paper 2 – Options exam paper. Two long-answer questions to be answered from two different sections. Chapters 4, 5, 6, 7 and 8 of this book. *For exam purposes, just study two chapters from this section.* Two hours.

Paper 3 – Unseen passage focusing on the application of qualitative methods. Three short answer questions, applying materials from chapter 9 of this book. One hour.

NOTES

NOTES

NOTES

IBDP REVISION COURSES

Summary

Who are they for?
Students about to take their final IBDP exams (May or November)

Locations include:
Oxford, UK
Rome, Italy
Brussels, Belgium
Dubai, UAE
Adelaide, Sydney & Melbourne, AUS
Munich, Germany

Duration
2.5 days per subject
Students can take multiple subjects

The most successful IB revision courses worldwide

Highly-experienced IB teachers and examiners

Every class is tailored to the needs of that particular group of students

Features

- Classes grouped by grade (UK)
- Exam skills and techniques – typical traps identified
- Exam practice
- Pre-course online questionnaire to identify problem areas
- Small groups of 8–10 students
- 24-hour pastoral care.

Revising for the final IB exams without expert guidance is tough. Students attending OSC Revision Courses get more work done in a shorter time than they could possibly have imagined.

With a different teacher, who is confident in their subject and uses their experience and expertise to explain new approaches and exam techniques, students rapidly improve their understanding. OSC's teaching team consists of examiners and teachers with years of experience – they have the knowledge and skills students need to get top grades.

The size of our Oxford course gives some particular advantages to students. With over 1,000 students and 300 classes, we can group students by grade – enabling them to go at a pace that suits them.

Students work hard, make friends and leave OSC feeling invigorated and confident about their final exams.

We understand the needs of IBDP students – our decades of experience, hand-picked teachers and intense atmosphere can improve your grades.

> "I got 40 points overall, two points up from my prediction of 38, and up 7 points from what I had been scoring in my mocks over the years, before coming to OSC. Thank you so much for all your help!"
>
> OSC Student

Please note that locations and course features are subject to change - please check our website for up-to-date details.

Find out more: osc-ib.com/revision   +44 (0)1865 512802